# Reminiscences

# ► of ◄

# Balls-Town:

## *Echoes and Whispers of Forgotten Legacies*

Amy Shannon

Amy Shannon
Essence Enterprises
Malta, NY 12020
https://essenceenterpriseus.com/

*ISBN Hardcover: 978-1-969718-11-3*
*ISBN Paperback 978-1-969718-12-0*
*LCCN: 2025921096*

Credits:
Cover Illustration Copyright © 2026 Cover design by Amy Shannon

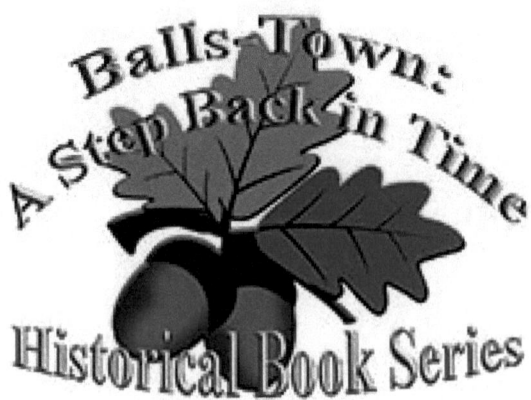

# About the Author

Amy Shannon is a legend keeper, storyteller, and historian whose roots run deep in upstate New York. A lifelong resident of the Capital Region, Albany, Schenectady, and Saratoga Counties. Amy calls the Ballston Spa/Malta area her true hometown, a place where she's planted her heart and built a life of meaning.

A mother of four, Amy, shares a close bond with three of her sons, each one a steadfast supporter of her creative journey. She is the founder of the acclaimed *Amy's Bookshelf Reviews*, a professional book reviewer, editor, author promoter, and host of the *Amy's Bookshelf Reviews* podcast on Spotify.

Amy's literary path began with full-length, dramatic, character-driven fiction. As her health shifted, so did her storytelling, toward short stories, children's books, and historical nonfiction. In 2024, she published *Balls-Town: A Community of History, Friends, Neighbors, and Lingering Spirits*, a tribute to the pioneers of Balls-Town that earned a spot on Amazon's historical best-sellers list.

Her article about Lucretia Booth, published in 2025, made her a local historian. It sparked a desire to save the lives of those forgotten, people from Balls-Town and nearby areas deserving more. Amy authored another article inspired by her second cousin, Bill, who is a Schenectady County historian, called *The Ballston Brief: The Law School That Time Misplaced.* It was published in November 2025.

Amy writes with a purpose: to honor, to remember, and to inspire. Her words are vessels of legacy, carrying stories forward so that no one is forgotten.

# Contents

# For Dad

*Dennis Earl Shannon*

*Where my stubbornness and poetic interest in history come from and will never fade.*
*A man of genius and poetry, and the continual quest for life and knowledge.*

# "Thank you!"

*A grateful "thank you" to my friend, Bill Hoolihan.*

*To my son, Robert, and his handsome husband, Darrin. My son, William. And my son Louis, and his beautiful wife, Freesia,*

*Thank you also to my cousin, Bill Buell, a historian himself, and for all his support.*

*I must also thank my fur baby, Flash. He is a cat that gives me support, and I always reciprocate. (And I can't forget our other animals, Tanj (kitty), Stanley (my beautiful female turtle), and Han (our bearded dragon). And of course, my grand fur babies ... Hyper (he's a cockapoo), and Wonton, Rangoon, and Noodle (my grand-guinea piggies); without them, life would be boring.*

*And to my friend, Quantum, whose quiet companionship and thoughtful insight helped m gather the scattered feathers of memory and arrange them into flight.*

# **Acknowledgements**

William Curtiss (descendant of the Curtisses) and member of the Ballston Spa Village Cemetery Association.
Susan Strange (descendant of the Booth family)
The Archives at the Albany Academy for Girls (in Albany, NY)

"Women belong in all places where decisions are being made."

-Ruth Bader Ginsberg


A quote that I have on my wall, and that inspires me to do more.

# Preface

This book began with footsteps, soft ones, careful ones, through old cemeteries with my mother, Sue, and my maternal grandmother, Rowena. We wandered among the stones, reading each name aloud, curious about them, and always searching for the oldest one. It seemed usual to me; it was revered. A quiet ritual passed down through generations, teaching me to listen to history with my feet on the earth and my heart open.

The stories in these pages are drawn from those walks, and from the archives I've come to know like old friends: newspaper clippings, mission boxes, supper menus, and obituaries. I am a contributor to FindAGrave.com, where I add memorials for those who are missing, link family members across generations, and update entries with the information I've gathered. When I cannot find someone, I do my best to ensure they are remembered and connected to their kin. Some women profiled here aren't even footnotes in history. So, I trace their families, listen to the echoes of those who loved them, and make careful, educated inferences about who they might have been.

Accuracy matters. I use multiple sources to confirm details, and when something cannot be verified, I make notes of it. Where photographs could not be found, I created silhouettes, so even in absence, their shadow leaves a mark. Not everyone had portraits or paintings made. Even those who held public office sometimes left no image behind. I found the few photos by chance, nestled in old books or concealed on trustworthy websites.

This book is a walk-through memory. Certain existences stretched out, while others ended in a flash of sadness. Some names are nearly forgotten; others still echo in local memory. I've included photos of headstones and gravesites not to mourn, but to remember. These stones are not just markers; they're echoes.

I've learned that even if you've never heard of someone, it doesn't mean their life didn't matter.

I hope this book is unlike any other you've read. It is a tribute to lives lived and lives unlived, a gentle light cast on lost shadows. It is my way of continuing the walk. I hope you'll join me.

Throughout this book, there are graphics used as dividers, but they are more than just dividers; they are symbols of the life that precedes the graphic.

| | |
|---|---|
| | Memorial for lost children. |
| | Memorial for Veterans |
| | Medical Doctors |
| | Justice of the Peace, Judges, Attorneys |
| | Educators |

*An additional note: there are a few references to a "common school." It was a public school intended to be free, publicly funded, and accessible to all children regardless of social class. These schools differed from seminaries and academies.*

# Welcome to the Past

**Reminiscences of Balls-Town: Echoes and Whispers of Forgotten Legacies** is not just a history book; it is a walkthrough memory, a quiet act of listening to the lives that shaped a community and those nearly lost to time.

Ingrained in generations of cemetery walks and guided by the author's deep commitment to reminiscence, this book brings together archival research, family lore, and poetic reflection. It honors the prankster sons and dedicated daughters, the women whose names barely made the records, and the children who never took a breath. Some left behind headstones; others left only whispers. All left a mark.

Through silhouettes where photos are missing, and carefully linked memorials on FindAGrave, the author restores connection across generations. Each story is a thread in the hidden tapestry of Balls-Town's past, woven from the stories of the lives and deaths of people, people that leave a mark, even if it's a grave marker, headstone, gravestone, a passing article in the newspaper, under "deaths" with a simple two-line obituary, or one with a deserving obituary, honoring their lives.

This is a book for those who believe that every life matters, that memory is an act of love, and that even the quietest voices deserve to be heard. It is a tribute to lives lived and unlived, a lantern held up to the shadows, and an invitation to walk beside the author in honoring the legacies etched in forgotten corners.

*Every life, every death has a story to tell, with the silent echoes of legacies.*

# Foreword

By Bill Buell
(Schenectady County Historian and my second cousin)

"I love to rove o'er history's page,
Recall the hero, and the sage;
Revive the actions of the dead,
And memory of ages fled."
-   Felecia Dorothea Hemans (1793-1835)

Amy Shannon's writing journey began with a love of poetry and a desire to learn more about her family genealogy. Fortunately for the rest of us, those endeavors blossomed into a powerful interest in her local community.

Put all those together, and we have a historian who isn't focused on the headlines and the names that dominate our New York State educational curriculum. Instead, Shannon focuses on the average American of bygone eras, and in her latest book, "Reminiscences of Balls-Town: Echoes and Whispers of Forgotten Legacies," the women aren't just an afterthought. The women lead the way.

You might recognize some of the last names; the Doubledays, the Gordons, the Taylors, the Wests and others, but of the women who married or were born into those families little is known, even for serious history buffs who call Ballston home. Thanks to Shannon's work, we now have a history of those wonderful women who, with just a cursory look, might be referred to as "average" or "typical." Shannon, however, argues convincingly that there is nothing average about most anyone, and that anyone's story is memorable, at times fascinating and important to revisit and to keep alive.

The inclusion of Martha Washington - the first First Lady of these United States of America - into the book seems to be a perfect fit. No, she wasn't a Ballstonian, but contrasting her life with "average" women makes perfect sense and is an interesting a short diversion from the rest of her subjects.

Anyone who enjoys reading history, especially local history and stories about family and community, will find this book a treat for readers of all ages. And while Balls-Town is in the title, this book is for anyone in Saratoga County, Schenectady County and Albany County, as well as the entire Capital Region.

In fact, as English poet Felicia Dorothea Hemans would suggest, it's for anyone, anywhere, who knows the value in looking back.

# Whispers: Women of Worth

*Stories of resilience, labor, and legacy, told silently, and quantum voices history overlooked.*

## *Women of Worth*

Standing strong, hand on her heart
deep breaths, long exhales,
Her strength never diminishes.
Her love and loyalty
for husband, for children
Celebrating the triumphs,
mourning the tragedies,
keeping home and hearth
keeping heart and soul
Oh, to mend a broken heart
Oh, to carry forward
Take his hand, smile and nod.
be seen and heard.
He listens.
He understands.
She stands beside him.
When the world wants
her behind him.
Keeping home and hearth
Toiling, cooking, baking
mending, sewing,
bookkeeping
Keeping house,
Keeping hearth.
-Amy Shannon 2025

## *Prologue of the Hearth*

Before history records the battles, the laws, the names of men, there is the rhythm of women's days. They rise with the fire; they labor through the hours; they return to quiet work when the world grows dim. Their lives are not written in ledgers or carved in stone, yet without them, no field would yield, no household would stand, no child would grow. This is the obscured inheritance of women: the pulse beneath the page, the breath behind the story.

All women are of worth, no matter the social status, race, culture or even whom they did or didn't marry. Each woman wakes up and starts her day. The only difference is where she wakes up, and what makes up her existence is now all about. Travel back in time and visualize the woman's every day.

## *Farmer's Wife*

Dawn breaks with the smell of wood smoke. She kneads bread while the baby stirs in the cradle. She rises early, tending the fire, preparing food, and milking the cows before the sun is high. Throughout the day she toils without stopping. As evening falls, she returns to peaceful work, sewing by lamplight, mending clothes, and preparing the family's main meal. Her influence is invisible, her name rarely written, though her hands sustained the household.

## *Prominent Socialite*

She wakes up in a brick townhouse, with the sound of carriage wheels on cobblestones. She rises too early, overseeing servants or managing the household accounts, ensuring children's tutors and meals are in order. Her day is filled with constant labor of a different kind, social calls, charitable teas, and maintaining a home that reflects her husband's standing. When night falls, she gets back to her silent work. Her legacy is unnoticeable.

## *The Gentlewoman*

Her day begins in a rented room, perhaps shared with another seamstress. She awakens before dawn, setting to work as a teacher, seamstress, or servant, her livelihood dependent on long hours of labor.

She heads downstairs to the shared supper area, where the tenants gather for breakfast before work. The housemother prepares the midday meal, a peaceful undertaking of care before the women disperse to their jobs. All day, she sews until her eyes tire or instructs children. At night she goes back to calm work.

Her legacy is unseen, precarious but independent, remembered only in ledgers and parish rolls, yet she carved out spaces for reform, for education, for a life shaped by quiet determination.

## *The Widow*

She awakens to the empty side of the bed, where he once lay. For a moment, silence, before the baby cries, before the children return from chores, before she must put on her best smile and begin the day. She rises early, already dressed in her calico gown, cradling the baby who still cries for papa. She cooks at the iron stove in the lean-to, surrounded by the aroma of wood and the memory of his hands in every plank and nail. Throughout the day she labors constantly, guiding her daughters as they bring in milk and eggs, preparing food for both the table and the general store. In the evening, she returns to quiet work, holding her children close, her husband's pipe still on the hearth, his coat still hanging by the door. Her legacy is unseen, carried in resilience, in the children's smiles that mask their grief, in the survival of a family built on memory and endurance.

## *The Dutiful Sister*

She wakes up in her sister's bed; her brother-in-law has already gone to seek work. Only months ago, her sister died in childbirth, leaving three children behind. She came to help after the funeral and never left. And her sister's children are now hers to care for. Now through the day she labors constantly, cooking, cleaning, and filling the space her sister once held, while her brother-in-law works to provide.

When he perceived her lasting devotion, he took her as his bride, and at only eighteen she became a partner and mother. In the evening, she returns to quiet work, rocking children who are not her own, dreaming of the child she may one day bear. Her legacy is unseen, a life of sacrifice, stepping into her sister's place not out of choice but of duty, embodying the quiet resilience expected of women.

# The Unseen Legacy of Women

## *Invisible Labor*

During the 1700s, 1800s, and far into the 1900s, a woman's value was often measured by her marital status. Single women got the name "spinsters," an expression loaded with shame, but they could, and were required to, earn a living. Their roles spanned domestic service, teaching, sewing, dressmaking, factory labor, and farm work. Ladies of elevated social status could work as governesses, while widowed women, defined by sorrow and hardship, had to maintain their households, especially with offspring to care for.

Married women bore the weight of domestic life. Their responsibilities, shaped by social class and their husbands' occupations, included managing the home, raising children, and performing endless chores. In farming families, where men often took on additional jobs to make ends meet, the burden of agricultural labor frequently fell to the women. Regardless of riches or station, a woman's work remained steady, crucial, and mostly unrecognized.

## *Legal Constraints and Erased Identity*

Until August 18, 1920, women in America could not vote. Even after suffrage, equality remained elusive. A woman could not own property unless she inherited it, and upon marriage, any assets she held became her husband's. She could not run for office, sign contracts, or keep her own wages. The legal doctrine of coverture erased her identity, folding her existence into her husband's.

Historical records reflect this erasure. Many women appear only in passing in a son's obituary, a father's military file, or as "Mrs." followed by her husband's full name. If her husband ran a business, she worked beside him, perhaps even harder than he did. These women left behind legacies that history overlooked. You didn't have to be a hero to matter. You just had to work hard.

## *High Society and the performance of Femininity*

In resort towns like Ballston Spa, social class shaped a woman's daily life. "Elite" ladies, those with wealth, frequently via kin or spouses, needed to show sophistication. Their rituals involved "taking of the waters" at the Sans Souci Hotel, where mineral springs were used for bathing, drinking, and herbal treatments. These rituals were both medicinal and social.

Fashion itself presented a display. Dresses for the morning were an outfit for promenades, where women walked to be noticed. Socializing occurred in hotel lounges and communal areas, while evening wear marked a shift in tone, carriage rides with suitors or husbands, grand balls, and formal dinners. Certain times brought female visitors.

## *Ordinary Women, Extraordinary Lives*

A "typical" woman was anything but ordinary. Married women raised children, managed households, and often worked alongside their husbands, especially in farming families. Their labor extended to cooking, cleaning, sewing, budgeting, and child rearing, often while pregnant or grieving the loss of a child. Sewing meant repairing and creating garments for the entire family. Handling the home finances needed thrift, resourcefulness, and grit.

Women's social lives were centered on church, community events, and informal gatherings. Ballston Spa had several churches, including the First Baptist Church, which hosted educational and social programs. Going to neighbors, shopping, and attending local events delivered crucial support networks. Letters exchanged between family members reveal the routine of daily life, mundane tasks, family health, and financial concerns, offering glimpses into the grounded, enduring strength of these women.

Many poor women worked as seamstresses, laundresses, or domestic servants in wealthier homes. Others ran small businesses from their kitchens and parlors. The old saying is valid: a woman's tasks are never finished.

## *Grief, Faith, and the Naming of Children*

Losing children happened often, many to diseases that weren't curable then, but now are, causing extreme sorrow. Families, rich and poor, young and old, mourned infants and young children, but the grief and despair never interfered with their responsibilities. It was common to give later children the names of those they had lost, occasionally reusing the same name, irrespective of Faith guided many families, with the belief that God would signal when to stop having children. In this cycle of birth, loss, and hope, women carried the emotional and physical weight of survival.

## *Progress, or the Illusion of It*

By the late nineteenth century, the Married Women's Property Acts had chipped away at the old order of coverture, granting wives the right to own property, keep their wages, and even enter contracts in their own names. Yet these legal reforms unfolded slowly, and the census of 1880 still consigned nearly every married woman to the occupation of "keeping house," a phrase that concealed the breadth of their labor. In kitchens, they cooked over coal stoves, hauled water, scrubbed and ironed laundry, tended gardens, canned produce, churned butter, and baked bread. In the rural stretches around Ballston Spa, their responsibilities expanded further, milking cows, feeding chickens, and working the fields during planting and harvest. Though their efforts sustained households and farms alike, recognition was scarce, and the promise of autonomy offered by the law was tempered by the enduring weight of custom and expectation.

## *Gentlemen & Husbands*

Some husbands married their wives primarily to have children and rely on them to manage all household duties. That's not to say these men didn't love their wives; many did, but what was required was obvious and firm. Other husbands supported their wives and children's education, hoping their daughters would receive the same opportunities as their sons.

Not all women could access the same educational or occupational experiences, but this never stopped them from fighting for their rights. Often, a husband had to put his name on any enterprise his wife wished to build, since she lacked the legal standing to do so herself. A man who absolutely loved and respected his wife extended that support and respect to their daughters, nurturing a legacy of empowerment.

Through every challenge and constraint, women's strength, love, and labor formed the foundation upon which families and communities endured. Their names may be absent from monuments, but their legacy is written in survival itself, the quiet architecture of day-to-day living, the unseen scaffolding of history.

# Lucretia Foot Booth (1804-1872) [1]

*Daughter, Mother, Wife, Educator, Visionary*

*Betsey Foot. Archives of the Albany Academy for Girls*

Lucretia Foot Booth was born in Troy, NY, on December 9, 1804. Lucretia's father and mother were Ebenezer Foot (1773–1814) and Betsey Colt Foot (1774–1847), and she was an only child.

Betsey Colt Foot, Lucretia's mother, one with strength, desired the finest schooling and possibilities for her daughter. Betsey was the primary influence for the start of the Union School for Girls in Albany, NY (now the Albany Academy). It was once two separate schools, one for girls and one for boys. Prompted by the lack of educational opportunities for her daughter, Lucretia, she encouraged her husband, Ebenezer, who was a lawyer, to draw up a charter for a new school that would provide girls with a classical education. Other families nearby gave them immense support, and the academy soon became a reality. Both sides of her family, the Foots and the Colts, were prominent families, served as the guiding force behind the establishment of the Union School for Girls in Albany. The Albany Academy for Girls originated in 1814 on the then-revolutionary notion that girls and women merit and can achieve advanced learning and socially involved existences.

*Silhouette of Ebenezer Foot at the Albany Academy for Girls*

[1] This sketch is an expanded version of an article written for Saratoga County (NY) Roundtable. https://www.newsbreak.com/news/4148930511893-the-educational-legacy-of-lucretia-foot-booth

In 2013, Louise Copeland Marks created a fictional version of Betsey's journal, called *To Elevate and Adorn the Mind.*

The Albany Institute of History & Art has a painting of Lucretia Foot as a child. The artist was not identified, and it was painted around 1806.[2]

*Lucretia Foot as a child*

## The Foots and The Colts

Lucretia was a family name; several ancestors and descendants carried that name. Mary Peck Foot and Captain John Foot were Ebenezer's parents. Ebenezer had four siblings: John, Mary, Lavinia, and Samuel. Betsey's parents were Benjamin Colt and Lucretia Ely. Betsey had six siblings: Lucretia [1], Daniel, Lucretia [2], Amey, Elisha, and Christopher.

## Lucretia and Lebbeus

In 1821, Lucretia married Lebbeus Booth (1784-1859). Together, they had twelve children; a few of the children died incredibly young. Lebbeus, with the urging and support of Lucretia, opened the first female seminary within Ballston Spa. When Lebbeus established the Ballston Spa Female Seminary, the local news wrote an article (circa 1825) article written, "The Female Seminary is under the superintendence of *Mr. Booth,* a gentleman who is eminently qualified for the undertaking, having been for several years the principal instructor in the female academy at Albany. The site of the institution is of a very pleasant and healthy eminence, commanding a view of the entire village, and the surrounding country for some distance. The building itself is spacious and airy and occupies with the out grounds and improvements, occupies upwards of an acre of land. This institution, though of recent establishment, has, from the well-known experience and celebrity of its proprietor, commanded a full share of patronage. They were educated here during the last season, about 40 females, from various parts of the state, and some from other states. Among the various branches taught are natural and moral philosophy, belles-lettres, chemistry, geometry and history; and when required, competent teachers instruct in the

---

[2] Archives of the Albany Academy for Girls

several branches of musick, drawing and dancing. The terms of tuition and board are quite reasonable; and the general management of the institution is spoken of in the highest terms of commendation."-[3]

Lebbeus, an intelligent man, gave support to his wife. When the school closed, he changed his interest in manufacturing and other business proprietorships. Lebbeus wore many hats for Saratoga County. He was a member of Christ Church. In 1840, he served as a loan commissioner for the county. In 1844, he worked as the county superintendent of the poor. He became director and vice president of the Ballston Spa Bank, and president of the Saratoga County Bible Society. He lived for 70 years.

Lucretia outlived her husband, and she lived sixty-eight years old. (For more details, see "The Booths")

---

[3] https://www.livingplaces.com/NY/Saratoga_County/Ballston_Spa_Village.html

# Clarissa Watson Horton (1780-1839)

*Daughter, mother, sister, proud and loyal in faith, and in heart.*

Clarissa, originated in Ballston, daughter of a Revolutionary War captain, lived through a transformative era. Still, akin to many females of her era, her narrative might have been integrated into

the periphery of her father's and son's legacies. Clarissa's mother and father were Captain Titus Watson and Mercy Merrill Watson. Raised with several siblings, she belonged to a family she adored and persevered in, with dignity and devotion.

Clarissa married into the Horton family upon her marriage to Ezekial II. Clarissa lived through the American Revolution, the War of 1812, and the early industrial age. She handled a household, nurtured children, and engaged in community affairs in Saratoga County. Ezekial survived fighting in the War of 1812.

Her son, James, grew up to be a prominent member of Ballston society, and he attended the *Ballston Spa Common School and Academy*. He married and later became the postmaster.

She probably handled a household, nurtured children, and engaged in community life in Saratoga County. Clarissa is in the 1830 US Federal Census indirectly, as women weren't mentioned individually. However, Ezekiel Horton is mentioned as head of household in Saratoga County, yet she was referred to as the "wife," but also listed several children or boarders. She had only one child. This backs the thought that Clarissa took part in the management of a household, possibly connected to the tavern or stables Ezekiel ran.

Despite no accounts of Clarissa or the Hortons belonging to a religious institution, Clarissa and her family had multiple possibilities to take part in church and their faith. James was a devoted Christian and a lifelong member of the Episcopal Church.

Based on her burial and her son's faith in Ballston Spa Village Cemetery, there's a good chance she had connections to the local Episcopal Church. Church women often played roles in hospitality, charity, and community organizing, especially in tavern-owning families. Clarissa may have hosted travelers, prepared meals, and helped run the business behind the scenes. Clarissa passed away at 59.

# Eliza Hoffman Walsh (1831-1869)

*Eliza lives beyond records and shadows, never forgotten.*

To this day, the life and death of Eliza are surrounded by mystery and ghost stories. Most of what is known about Eliza's life is that she was orphaned at an early age and raised by her mother's sister, Sarah Burtis La Dew, and Sarah's husband, John C. F. Ladew, an Albany meat merchant. She was married to Edward Lewis Walsh. Walsh owned gambling houses in Saratoga and the City of New York and was a friend of John Morrissey, who built Saratoga's Casino, and he was a gambler himself, indeed a "high roller."

In 1870, a year after Eliza's death, a crypt was built in the Ballston Spa Village Cemetery. It was among the original crypts established in the cemetery. For years, the place was thought to be Eliza Walsh's crypt, where she rested. Facing Ballston Avenue, the free-standing vault carries the date, 1870, on top of its stone. Chiseled in the second block is "E. L. WALSH." The initials could either be Eliza's or her husband, Edward's.

Around the period of the vault's creation, the remains of Eliza's mother, who passed away at thirty during delivery, plus a ten-year-old sister were taken out of the ground and moved near the crypt. The aunt and uncle and Eliza's brother, a noted gambler, and his wife are buried behind the vault. It would be a family grouping, except Eliza is missing, or so it seems.

For generations, a ghost story has been repeated that a couple would appear at the crypt for dining inside.

Several years ago, it was to be known that the crypt was empty. There are no remains in the crypt, and no signs of what happened to either Edward or Eliza.

Author's Note: I thought it kind to place a section in this book that detailed the life of Eliza Hoffman Walsh and was examined beyond its cryptic ghost story. However, the only information found on Eliza was what I have included in her biography sketch. A search of any gravesite database, or other searches for Eliza, are only about the lore surrounding her death, and afterwards. I use findagrave.com, and the crypt is listed as E.L Walsh, and everything is listed as unknown, so much so that I could not even leave a virtual flower for Eliza.

Even though no records show her end or where she is buried, and the location of her remains is a secret, Eliza's family was put to rest in a crypt built thoughtfully. She belongs in this book not as a ghost but as a remembered person. More than a story of absence, Eliza, wherever her body, mind, and soul now reside, is not forgotten.

*Crypt is listed as E.L Walsh*

*Resting place of the Ladews*

# Ella "Cuddy" Booth (1853-1915)

## *A Quiet Force of Civic Grace*

Born in Ballston Spa, Ella Marion inherited more than a name; she carried forward the legacy of Lucretia Foot Booth, her grandmother. Lucretia was a woman whose strength and resolve echoed through generations. Raised in a family rooted in early American ideals, Ella grew into a person of quiet influence, navigating the shifting tides of the post-bellum society with grace and conviction. Ella's parents were John Chester Booth and Margaret Booth. Her young sister, Mattie, died from diphtheria at seven. The 1855 survey shows that John, Margaret, and Ella, aged 2, lived with her grandparents.

John died young, at age 28, and before he passed away, he started compiling a history of Saratoga County. Later, Ella gave permission to author Edward Grose, who added John's work in the "Centennial History of the Village of Ballston Spa."

Though history has offered few headlines in her name, Ella's presence in Towanda, Pennsylvania, was anything but invisible. People recognized her as a notable citizen, a saying that, during her era, frequently hid how much a woman achieved. Ella, a teacher, seemed fitting given her background. She was determined to give every child a proper and comparable education, no matter gender. Whether through education, civic engagement, or the nurturing of community bonds, Ella Booth shaped the moral and cultural fabric of her town. Her life bridged eras: from the horse-drawn rhythms of antebellum America to the industrial hum of the early 20th century.

She is one of a multitude of women whose names history includes, while their influence merits prominence. Ella Booth lived a life of substance, and in remembering her, we reclaim a piece of the truth: that prominence is not measured by fame, but by the depth of one's contribution to others.

When she died, she was laid to rest in Woodlawn Cemetery in the Bronx, a final resting place among many of New York's storied souls. But Ella's true legacy lies not in stone, but in the lives, she touched, the values she upheld, and the modest strength she embodied.

# Jane Gates Blood Parkinson (1812–1894)

## *The Quiet Matriarch of Bloodville*

Jane Gates was born in Ballston Spa. When she grew up, she met and married Isaiah Blood, who followed his father, who owned a business and a large parcel of land. After Isaiah and Jane married, they lived in a modest home on the land once called the Hamlet of Bloodville. Isaiah Blood was the owner and operator of the factories that manufactured axe and scythes.

"THE MAPLES," BLOODVILLE. HOME OF ISAIAH BLOOD NOW THE HOME OF HIS GRAND-SON, WM. H. KNICKERBACKER.

The Bloods allowed their employees and their families to have homes in Bloodville, so they had a place to live, and a place to work. Although limited information is available regarding Jane, she played a significant role in the Bloodville community and was recognized as a prominent and respected figure within Ballston Spa society circles.

The Bloods, Jane and Isaiah, built a legacy in the community, with Jane serving as a significant figure in the village's social and economic landscape. The couple had one child, William. Unfortunately, the Bloods lost their son William when he perished in the creek that powered his father's scythe factory. He was just five years old.

Even with such a tragedy, the Bloods continued working and taking care of the employees and their families. Jane assisted her husband in any way possible, since they were allies, despite a lack of formal agreement.

Many times, women pioneers and settlers do not have a lot written about them or their accomplishments. It is important to remember that history comprises legacies that could be forgotten. Some might be unfamiliar with Isaiah Blood or Bloodville; it's one of the industrial sites created near streams, which came together to provide energy for the factories.

Jane stood by her husband when he entered politics. Isaiah was voted into the Assembly and State Senate from the Saratoga district in 1839 and again in 1869. New York's Governor Morgan appointed him to be a member of the war committee to help recruit soldiers for the Civil War.

While Isaiah built scythe and axe empires and served in the New York State Senate, Jane held the pulse of Bloodville, a hamlet named for her husband but sustained by her modest stewardship.

After Isaiah's death in 1870, Jane married William John Parkinson, yet she remained in Bloodville until her passing in 1894. He raised her daughter, Helen, from her second marriage there. Her daughter Helen married Henry Knickerbocker.

Jane's obituary noted her as "a woman of rare dignity and kindness," though few records detail her personal voice. That silence is precisely what makes her story powerful: she lived through fires, wars, and the rise and fall of a manufacturing dynasty, all while shaping the domestic and social rhythms of a town that bore her name.

Henry Knickerbocker managed the business for 20 years. The factories burned and were ruined. The employees and their families moved to find other work. The Bloodville legacy and the Blood bloodline ended with the passing of Helen and Henry's sons, William and Henry Jr.

*Jane's final resting place*

# Julia Stone Crandell Shields (1850-1921)

## *Wife, Mother, Daughter, Heir, Survivor*

If you live in Ballston Spa long enough, you may hear about the "haunted" Crandell House, and the

ghost stories about Sylvester Crandell (maybe only knowing his last name) walking around the cupola of his home. But this is not about Mr. Crandell, the murdering husband of Julia Stone Crandell. It's about Julia herself.

Julia was a divorced mother of Julie Bulkeley, who was wealthy, as her father left her and her mother a substantial wealth portfolio. Something that drew in the likes of Crandell. That is his end. On December 19, 1887, he killed himself after shooting his wife's family, killing her mother and her daughter, and injuring Julia, who had life-threatening injuries, but she survived.

Now, take a step back. Julia was the daughter of Mary and Samuel Stone. Mr. Stone was a paper collar manufacturer. She married Cassius Bulkeley in 1870, who was an insurance broker. The couple had Julie, and later Julia filed for divorce of Cassius, and it was granted. Julia came from a successful family, and they were very wealthy. Samuel Stone died in 1866, 21 years before the incident. Julia was strong like her mother, and a formidable woman. All the women in Julia's family were strong women. Crandell was a colleague of her first husband and seemed to be successful as well. The fortune was controlled by Mary Stone, Julia's mother. Both Mary and Julia were very well-educated women and controlled their household finances. This did not sit well with Crandell.

Crandell had a tough time keeping a job and managing his own money, yet he was a debt collector and financially savvy. When Crandell married Julia, he was not just married to Cassius's ex-wife but lived in his home and slept in his bed. Back then, this was very improper, and even their Reverend, Dr. Irvin, refused to marry the couple.

Crandell pressured Julia to get her mother to give her the entire inheritance and take control of her father's property. Julia left it in her mother's capable hands. Crandell's intention was about love but was more about fortune. He had a habit of living beyond his means. Crandell ended up living with his mother-in-law, his wife, and stepdaughter.

When the Crandells moved to Ballston Spa, they bought the "family mansion." It was a former residence of Colonel B. F. Baker, who built it, furnished it, and maintained the five acres of land. It is a three-story home, and because of its position, there is a splendid view of the village of Ballston Spa. Mrs. Stone eventually sold her own home and had another built. She sold the house to Mr. Thomas Shields. In the spring of 1887, she moved in with her daughter, her granddaughter, and Mr. Crandell.

It was rumored, and yet probably the truth, that the two fought incessantly over money, and Crandell was often seen by himself in the house's cupola, pacing.

In 1887, Crandell entered the kitchen, where Mary (Mrs. Stone), Julia, and young Julia were eating breakfast. Once he shot, the women ran from the table to the kitchen, while he ran after them, still shooting. His focus was on Mary. He saw Rebecca (Mrs. Ellis) and shot at her but missed. Mary ran from the house and fell into the snow, dying from her gunshot wound to the breast. He then reloaded his revolver and shot young Julia at close range. He then shot his wife, Julie, who received three wounds in the groin. Then Sylvester went up to the cupola and shot himself. Mrs. Ellis was uninjured. Even when he kept shooting at her, she escaped ran for help. The doctors of the town heard her cries for help, and entered the scene.

Though they thought Julia would die from her injuries, she survived. This happened on the weekend because on Monday morning, Julia was planning to go to Troy with her daughter, mother, and aunt in order to consult with their attorney. Crandell had a history of abuse toward Julie and Julia.

Crandell was buried in the Hortonfield Cemetery (now the Ballston Spa Village Cemetery). Mary and Julie were buried in Troy, at the Oakwood Cemetery. Julia, and her aunt, Mrs. Ellis, got help for them. Though her injuries were severe, and the consensus was that she would not live, however, she survived. She was clearheaded when she told the authorities what had happened. Julia lived a full life and married a third husband, Mr. Thomas Shields, in 1895. She had two stepdaughters. Thomas lived until 1903. Julia lived to the age of 70, having a lengthy illness and died in 1921. Julie didn't just survive;

she lived.

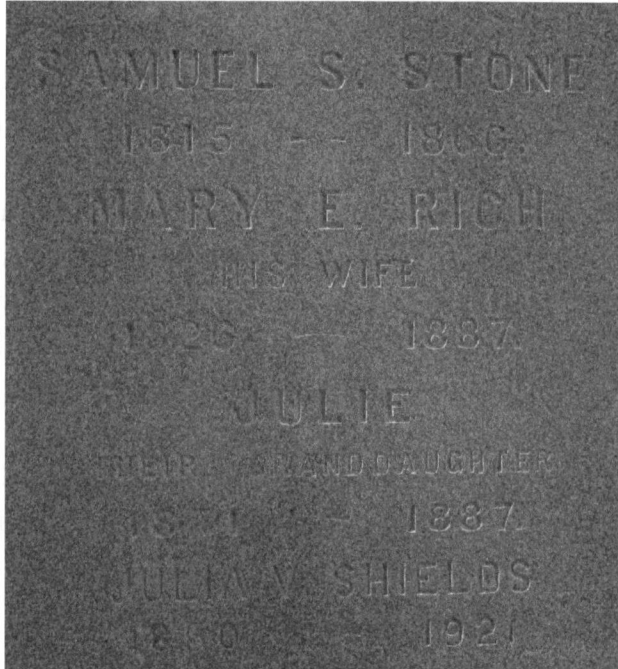

## A FATAL FAMILY QUARREL

A Terrible and Bloody Tragedy Enacted at Ballston Spa.

### SUICIDE OF THE MURDERER

S. S. Crandell, a Lawyer and Real Estate Broker, Takes Revenge With a Revolver in Wholesale Style and Then Kills Himself.

TROY, Dec. 19.—S. S. Crandell, formerly a lawyer and real estate broker in Troy, to-day shot his wife, his mother-in-law Mrs. S. S. Stone; his step-daughter, Julia Bulkley, and himself at their home in Ballston Spa. They are all dead but Mrs. Crandell, and she is dying. Mr. Crandell and his wife had a quarrel over money matters. Mrs. Crandell was the divorced wife of Crandell's legal associate. Crandell was once a candidate for a county office and was defeated. He was extravagant to his habits. His wife had money and the quarrel was over its control.

The place known as the Colonel Baker place was bought by Mrs. Stone about a year ago. The family consisted of Mrs. Stone, her sister, Mrs. Crandell and her son-in-law, Crandell. Mrs. Stone was about 62 years old. Her husband, S. S. Stone, was a large paper collar maker in Troy, and died several years ago, leaving a large property. The daughter refused to accept any property while her mother was alive. The daughter, Julia V. Crandell, was 37 years old. She has one child, the girl, Julia Bulkley.

It is said Crandell represented himself to be wealthy and worth $40,000 and finally married Mrs. Bulkley. Their married life has been unhappy. Mr. Crandell was in the habit of urging his wife to get the two-thirds of the Stone property which she owned and of which her mother had the use. She refused to do so. The trouble culminated yesterday, when Crandell and Mrs. Stone had a dispute as to the occupation of a workingmen employed on the place. At that time he called his wife several hard names, when she retorted that he was only a pauper, and had no property except what they gave him, he replied that she would be poorer before she was richer. A week ago the grandchild had made a complaint to have Crandell arrested for his abuse. It was on Sunday agreed that the ladies would go to Troy Monday and consult R. H. McClellan, their attorney.

The family, except Mrs. Ellis, were at the table eating breakfast this morning when Crandell began shooting. The ladies ran from the table to the kitchen, and he ran after them, firing across the room. His spite seemed to be against Mrs. Stone. He fired promiscuously among the others and at Mrs. Ellis. Mrs. Stone ran out of doors into the snow some rods from the house. He followed her to the door and shot after her. She fell exhausted into the snow and died soon after, a bullet in her breast showing the ball to have been fired in the house.

Crandell then turned about, loaded his revolver and, at short range, fired at Julia. The shot took effect near the navel. It was fired so close that a white spots she wore was burned by the powder. Mrs. Crandell received two wounds in the groin. Crandell then ran from the room and was not seen again until his dead body was found in the cupola of the house.

Mrs. Ellis at once raised an alarm and the people soon came flocking to the scene. It was too late to be of any assistance. Officers were placed in charge of the rooms and no one outside was admitted. A coroner was notified and a telegram sent to Attorney McClellan of Troy.

EVENING.—Mrs. Crandell, the fourth victim of S. S. Crandell's revolver, is still very weak. The two women will be buried at Oakwood Cemetery in this city. Crandell's remains will be interred at Ballston, where the tragedy occurred.

A coroner's jury viewed the remains of the three who are dead and the inquest was adjourned until Thursday. Another wound was discovered in Mrs. Crandell's body, making three in all. She is still alive.

CRANDELL'S MOTHER A PAUPER.

NEW BEDFORD, Mass., Dec. 19.—The mother of S. S. Crandell, the Troy lawyer who committed murder and suicide, is an inmate of the alms house in this city. Crandell refused to do anything for her relief.

## THE CRANDELL TRAGEDY INQUEST.

The Verdict of the Jury—Mrs. Crandell's Statement—Mrs. Ellis and the Drs. Lawrence Repeat their Experiences — The Case Judicially Closed.

Coroner Keifer, of Mechanicville, continued the inquest in the Crandell murder case in the court house on Saturday evening. Following is the *ante-mortem* statement of Mrs. Julia E. Crandell, which she made a few hours after the tragedy and while she was in an almost dying condition:

Am the wife of Sylvester S. Crandell, deceased; reside in the town of Milton, Saratoga county. About 7.30 a. m. of December 19th was sitting at the breakfast table; Mrs. Stone and myself were going to Troy; Mr. Crandell came in, sat down at the table and exclaimed: "Now is my time." He then drew a revolver out of his pocket and shot at me. He then shot at Mrs. Stone, shot again at me and then again at Mrs. Stone who ran out of the house calling for help, and I ran after her. He shot again at Mrs. Stone out of the door and also at me while outside. He then went back and shot my daughter, Julia Stone Bulkeley, in the butler's pantry. Mrs. Stone fell by the clothes reel in the yard, face down, about fifty feet from the house. Mrs. Ellis picked her up and brought her near the house; I was lying in the snow near the back piazza; Julia was lying in the hall. Crandell came back and went into the front part of the house and that was the last I saw of him.

Dr. E. S. Lawrence was sworn as to his discovery and the condition of the dead and wounded on that morning. Dr. H. W. Lawrence also testified professionally. Mrs. Rebecca Ellis, sister of Mrs. Stone, was present and related the incidents of that frightful tragedy, but nothing materially new was brought to light. After a brief deliberation the jury brought in and subscribed to the following verdict:

We, the undersigned jury, after hearing the evidence in the Crandell inquest and deliberating thereon, find that Mrs. Mary E. Stone, S. S. Crandell and Miss Julia S. Bulkely came to their death in the town of Milton, December 19th, 1887, at about 7.30 a. m., by reason of pistol shot wounds, said pistol being in the hands of Sylvester S. Crandell.

# Louisa Rose West (1822–1902)

*She held what history forgot and loved without applause.*

Louisa Rose was born in Exeter, England. She married George West in February 1840. The couple emigrated from England to America. They were the parents of five sons and one daughter. They lived in Tyringham, Massachusetts, and then moved to Ballston Spa, where they built a life and a forever home.

Many wives of the era found themselves dutifully silent, except within private, or having to show the public how dutiful a wife she could be, especially when George held seats in politics. Though little was written about her, Louisa's dedicated presence beside George throughout the Paper Mill's growth speaks volumes about her character.

Louisa remained at her husband's side as he and their son, George Jr., nurtured the family Paper Mill. She raised their children with unwavering devotion, mourning the babies they lost without breaking. After the heartbreaking death of infant Charles at nine months, and two other unnamed sons, she found the strength, without hesitating, to welcome more life into their family. Walter was often a troublesome son and man, yet his mother's steady hand was always there to guide him, even when he didn't listen. George and Louisa celebrated the birth of their daughter, Florence Louise, and with her name, she honored her mother.

She bore the challenges of her husband's political career with courage and strength, standing by him through its close. She aided her husband's return to the family business, and after George died, she died almost immediately after. She passed away in Saratoga at 79, and she rests in Ballston Spa Village Cemetery, in the family plot.

# Margaret Lee Powell (1832-1917)

*Devoted daughter, sister, mother, wife, and socialite.*

Margaret was born into the distinguished Ballston family, the Lees. Her parents were Edward Wescott Lee and Anna Maria Williams. She was a prominent member of the Ballston Society. She lived in Ballston Spa, Milton, and later, Saratoga Springs. She married Frederick Powell in 1865. The couple had two children, Alice Thompson Powell Luther and Harry Lee Powell.

In the 1907 *Centennial History of the Village of Ballston Spa* book by Edward Grose, she was mentioned in the Author's preface, stating "Acknowledgment is also due to Miss Winifred Taylor, of Freeport, Illinois, Mrs. Martha Seelye of NY, Mrs. Margaret Powell, Mrs. John Ford, Mr. Stephen Medbery and Mr. James Peckham of Ballston Spa, and Mrs. Mary Osborn and Mr. Willard Lester, of Saratoga Springs for valuable information furnished the author; to Mr. N. B. Sylvester, and Col. Wm. Stone for many interesting facts gathered from their historical writings, and to Mr. Enos Mann's "Bench and Bar of Saratoga County." Also, to Mr. J. S. Wooley, Feeney Brothers and Mr. N. L. Allcott for a number of illustrations."

She was also commended in the book for being a part of the "Ladies Committee" to help put together the Centennial, which was the celebration of Ballston Spa Village's incorporation.

Her passing occurred in Saratoga at the age of 85, with interment at Ballston Spa Village Cemetery.

# Martha Dandridge Custis Washington (1731-1802)

*Daughter, Widow, Mother, and the (first) First Lady (Lady Washington)*

*1Martha Curtis Washington*

Martha Dandridge was born on her parents' tobacco plantation. Though her family wasn't wealthy, Martha was taught how to behave as a woman of means. She was educated, but even so, it didn't match the education her brothers were able to receive. She may not have lived in Balls-Town, but she travelled with her husband, General Washington during the Revolutionary War, which played an integral part in Balls-Town history. Her contribution earns her a place in this book.

Martha, a wealthy widow, married George Washington when he was only a colonel in 1759. Martha had four children from her previous marriage to Daniel Parke Custis (1711-1751); Daniel, Frances, John "Jacky" who was a planter and a politician, and Martha (1756-1773). Each child had the name Parke for their middle name, which was the only way they would get their rightful inheritance from their father's passing.

Martha was a widow when she was only 26 years old, and she inherited a large estate. Daniel Parke Custis was the son of a wealthy planter in Virginia. When he passed, the total inheritance amounted to approximately $33,000, 17,000 acres of land, and hundreds of slaves. The legal and financial matters of the inheritance were a burden on Martha, as she had to raise her two surviving children, and grieve for the losses of her husband, two children, and her father. She was also left with the responsibility of managing the farmland and overseeing the well-being of the slaves.

Martha met George at a social in Williamsburg, and they courted during his leaves from the military. Martha married George in 1759 and moved to his plantation. Before George Washington even considered being a president, he was a military man and a bachelor. He never had children of his own, but he treated Martha's children as if they were. When Martha married George, she was one of the wealthiest widows in the Thirteen Colonies. They were married for forty years, and their relationship showed mutual respect and prioritized family and image above everything else.

During the Revolutionary War, Martha followed her husband from camp to camp, creating relief

efforts for the soldiers by feeding them, providing medicine and clothing. She played a motherly role for all the soldiers, and then her only surviving child, John Park Custis, died from an illness he contracted in one of the camps during the war.

After the conflict ended, she considered retirement a sanctuary in Mount Vernon, yet when George became the initial leader of America, she had to take on a more social function, as the leader's spouse, and it made her a public figure, a situation that never suited her. She knew she had to be dignified, and to poise humility that came with the governmental office. It represented unfamiliar terrain for all, especially post-war, getting freedom from British governance, and then transitioning to a government with a President for the start. After George retired, they moved to Mount Vernon in 1797. She persisted as a President's spouse, and she spent a considerable amount of her time meeting and greeting admirers and advising present or future first ladies.

When her husband died, she sealed his death chamber and study and never entered it again. She slept in an attic room, where she could look over her husband's burial site. Martha died in 1802, but she is still as well-known as her husband, the first President of America.

# Melinda Gordon VerPlanck Waller (1779-1857)

*A woman of legacy and legend, born within the founder's family.*

Melinda was the cherished daughter of James Gordon, a military general, and Mary Ball Gordon.

Her grandfather was Eliphalet Ball, the founder of Balls-Town. Melinda Gordon married William Beekman VerPlanck, son of Philip VerPlanck and Effie Beekman, in 1798. Together, they had three children: Mary Ann Catherine, William Gordon, and Philip Alexander, who was named after her younger brother.

Melinda married Henry Waller in 1806, after her first husband's death. Together, they had six children: Elizabeth, Melinda, Elizabeth Martina, Henry, Joseph, William, Mary and James.

This is a transcribed document based on Mrs. Waller's story about "Burning of Balls-Town" on the 16th of October 1780, conversing with Hon. George Scott, September 10, 1846.[4]

*"I was then nearly four years old, and my father, mother and myself slept in bed, in the room on the south side of the house, the room was the whole depth of the house with a window in the east and west end. That night before retiring, my mother had entreated my father to go over to Grandfather Ball's and stay, and to leave her as she was not afraid of being injured. A hint had been conveyed through some friendly tory source that he was in danger.*

*He refused, saying he would not be so cowardly as to go off and leave his wife and child. These were the last words he uttered before the enemy arrived. "We were awakened by the breaking of both the windows in the room and looking up saw a number of muskets with bayonets protruding into the room. My father arose and, in his shirt, went to the hall door, and opening it he found the hall filled with armed men and Indians. As he opened it a large Indian lifted his tomahawk and as it was descending, his arm was caught by Munro or Frazer, I forget own left.*

---

[4] The transcription is as it was written, except for punctuation edits to make it more readable.

*My father, seeing Stow lay dead as he was marched along, got permission to send back one of the servants under guard, with a message to mother to go immediately to her father's, as he was afraid some stragglers would return. She had just returned from the kitchen when she found a straw bed on fire and a fire-brand thrust into it. She extinguished the fire. The guard who came back with the message*

*discovered "Liz," who had just returned from the cornfield. He exclaimed, 'You huzzy, why are you not along with the rest of the company?'*

*Mother in reply asked him if he was so barbarous as to take a naked woman along. He told 'Liz' to find some clothes and put them on in a hurry. 'Liz' stepped out of the room but did not return in time to go along. "I recollect of being in my father's arms out of the door in the moonlight, when he stood under the charge of Langdon. I recollect awakening some time afterwards by the side of a log heap, in company with my mother and 'Liz,' where they had hid themselves. "When the prisoners were assorted above the Kayaderosseras, and Major Munro had given his bloody orders, they marched along in Indian file, each prisoner placed between two of the enemy. My father afterwards told me that the second man in front of him was Captain Collins, then a British soldier, then my father, and immediately behind him a strapping Indian, whether it was the same one who attempted to tomahawk him at the house I am not certain.*

*My father heard the soldier in front of him (he was a German somewhat in years) say to Captain Collins, 'I have been through all the wars in Europe and in a great many battles, but I have never before heard of such bloody orders as these. 1 can kill in the heat of battle but cannot be made to murder in cold blood. You need not fear me, for I will not obey the orders. But that Indian behind is thirsting for Gordon's blood, and the moment a gun is fired, Gordon is a dead man.' My father assured me, as well be imagined, that he expected the tomahawk in his head every moment during the whole day. "At Montreal, the prisoners on the first night were lodged in the Recollect Convent, a very filthy place.*

*The next morning my father was covered with vermin. James, Robert and Sanders Ellice, three brothers, Tories, one or more of whom had formerly lived in Schenectady, and were Indian which. My father was acquainted with both and had befriended them. He was then led out of the door and put under guard. One Langdon had charge of him. "The Indians, male and female, both were along, commenced pillaging. They took every article of clothing they could find, my father sent word for his clothes, but they were already secured. My mother was obliged to borrow from one of the blacks some articles of clothing, as she had nothing of her 'Ellice and Gordon had been formerly connected in trade at Schenectady. traders, and with whom my father was well acquainted, now lived in Montreal.*

*My father, the next morning, sent for James Ellice, who bailed him out of prison for three thousand pounds, and he stayed at his house afterwards. But Ellice having at his house much company, all hostile to the American cause, my father explaining to Ellice the reason, left his house and boarded with a Jew named Levy. Soon afterwards, for some cause which he could never ascertain, he was transferred to Quebec and confined in the 'Prove' Here he remained several months in close confinement. He was furnished with books and writing materials, and wrote out the translation of a French work, the manuscript of which I-now have. He was subsequently moved to the Isle of Orleans, where he found Judge White, the two Banta's, Enoch Wood, John Higby, Cassidy, and Cozzo, a Frenchman, and another person whose name I forget. He had occasionally drawn on ... for money which was fully paid. He saved the most of it, which (being 41) neighborhood, the father Gonzalez frankly ex gold) was concealed about his person.*

*On the island, they were put upon their patrol but confined at night. At this they remonstrated, but for no purpose. Believing their patrol was not in force during confinement, they escaped by night by means of a fisherman's boat, which they took without being able to compensate the owner. "Before reaching a settlement in Maine they had for several days gone without victuals. My father, famished and weak, gave out and lay down. The residue went on with an understanding that as soon as a settlement (which from indications they believed to be near) should be discovered, three guns should be fired. Soon after he heard the guns and was so excited that he sprang up and fell down three times in succession, in his haste to get there. The party soon returned and conducted him to the settlement.*

*With their hatchets, they constructed a raft on which they floated down the river (Kennebec). At one time the raft came in contact with some obstacle, by means of which my father was knocked into the river and sank to the bottom, but coming up near the hind end, was assisted on board. At another time during his starvation, he ate of some berries which nearly occasioned his death. Some of the time they subsisted on a kind of muscle. They finally reached Passamaquoddy Bay and thence went to Boston. Peace was established about the time they arrived home. The other prisoners after peace were taken to Halifax and thence to Boston."*

Melinda died at 78 years old. Melinda's death came in Brooklyn, far from the Gordon and Ball family plots of Ballston Spa. It is possible that she is buried in Green-Wood Cemetery in Greenwood Heights, NY, the same cemetery where her son Joseph Waller was buried. It is uncertain where she was put to rest, and yet, her presence endures in the lineage of the Gordons and Balls, and in the legacy of the Wallers.

# Sally Taylor Holmes (1792-1889)

*Guided by faith, she supported many while raising children and standing by her husband.*

Sally, daughter of Justice John and Chloe Taylor, similarly to her brothers and sisters, received an excellent education. Sally always seemed lively and happy, but since she was small for her size, some perceived her as weak and breakable. However, her family knew better. Her brother, John Taylor,

Sally Taylor Holmes

became a judge, and was very close to his sister. She was born in Saratoga County, but when she married Daniel Holmes in 1811, they moved to Lake Ontario. Though she no longer lived in Saratoga County, she was a formidable woman, who remained a woman of historical presence, along with her (locally famous and honored) family, the Taylors.

Daniel worked as a farmer and moved his family to "Holland Purchase," Wilson, NY, on the shore of Lake Ontario, where she had to endure the hardships and poverty of being a farmer's wife. She kept her faith, and stayed true to herself, encountering and surviving any emergency, physical, mental, and moral.

She was the parent of thirteen children, and ten lived to become family leaders. Sally's heart and hand remained available to the sad, sick, and needy. She was among a group of six in 1819, establishing the First Presbyterian Church of Wilson. To the church, her family, and neighbors, her sympathy, prayers, and material aid have been constantly and cheerfully given for sixty-seven years. She always gave a bountiful Thanksgiving dinner to her children and descendants every year for over fifty years, and yet, she never neglected expressing her earnest desire for the spiritual welfare of her family to the latest generation.

Her brother, Honorable John W. Taylor, in 1845 wrote: "She was a favorite sister. To energy and decision, she united a mild temper and great industry. She had a place for everything, and everything in its place." When over eighty years old, she was relating to a niece many of the incidents of her life and closed thus … and I think I have enjoyed as much domestic happiness as is often found on earth."

DANIEL HOLMES    MRS. DANIEL HOLMES

She occupied the old homestead with her daughter, Mary Elizabeth Holmes Brown, and family and was ready to welcome the absent members of the family and their friends. In 1886, she was in good health, wrote a beautiful letter, and was an industrious Bible student.

Sally raised their children, which was her role as a wife and mother. Her offspring, relatives, and faith created her world.

Sarah Ann (1812–1864) was the first child of Sally and David. In time, she married Nathaniel Emmons Davis, born in 1807, and together they built a life ingrained by family and devotion. Over the years, they welcomed seven children into their home: Samuel, Nathaniel Jr., Henry, Eliza, Daniel, Mary Elizabeth, and Luther. Sarah Ann passed away in 1864, leaving behind a legacy carried forward by her children and the serene strength of her marriage to Nathaniel, who lived until 1883.

Richard Cox (1813–1887) married Betsy Frost, born in 1819, and they nurtured two sons together: William Howard and Richard. After Betsy's passing in 1870, Richard found companionship again with Annista until he passed away. Through both relationships, Richard's life was marked by enduring family ties and resilience.

John Taylor (1815–1891) was named in tribute to his uncle. He lived for 76 years, a life defined by family and continuity. In 1836, he wed Mary Ann Pratt, and together they raised three children: Marietta, Elizabeth Ann, affectionately called "Lizzie" and John Jr. Through his namesake son and the enduring bonds of kinship, John's legacy carried forward, ingrained in both tradition and love.

William Edward (1817–1824) lived six years, long enough to capture the heart of his family, but not long enough to grow up and spread his wings.

Dr. Ezra Sprague (1819–1914), a person with healing and endurance, passed the age of 95, spending his life committed to the practice of medicine. He married Orienna Elizabeth Robbins, and together they raised four children: Arthur, Chloe, Rosa Minerva, and Victor Augustus. Ezra's long life spanned nearly a century of change, and through his work and family, he left a legacy of care and commitment.

James Leander [1] (1822–1824) lived two years. Though his time was short in life, his spirit forever belongs to his mother's heart.

Elisha Taylor (1824–?) married Adah Davenport on New Year's Day in 1849, and together they raised a family of at least four children, two sons and two daughters. Elisha spent much of his life in Wilson, New York. But then, he and his wife passed away. Their modest presence and family ties added to the enduring legacy of the Holmes lineage.

George Alfred (1826–1907) lived for 81 years, a span marked by steady devotion and family ties. George married Elizabeth Remele, and together they welcomed one son, George Alfred Jr., into their lives. Although their family was not large, the identity and existence of George moved onward into the coming generation, a faint reflection of the Holmes bloodline.

Mary Elizabeth (1828–1903) lived for 75 years, a span marked by family devotion and sober strength. Mary married James Glen Ogilvie Brown, and together they raised four children: Edward Delavan, Mary Elizabeth, Joseph Elmer, and Llewellyn. Through her children and the enduring bond of her marriage, Mary's legacy continued to echo gently through the generations.

James Edward (1831–1888) served in the conflict of the American Civil War, a chapter of his life that marked him with courage and sacrifice. In 1853, James married Sarah Hyde. Together, they raised two children: Harry, born in 1861, and Hattie, born in 1867. James died in 1888 at 57 and found his final resting place in Woodland Cemetery in Des Moines, Iowa. Sarah lived until 1912, reaching the age of 81. Their lives, shaped by war, family, and quiet endurance, remain part of the Holmes family's enduring legacy.

Daniel Jr. (1833–1908) lived for 75 years, a life marked by silent constancy and familial devotion. Daniel married Laura Rudd Spencer, and together they had one son, Harry Porter. Through this single branch, the Holmes name continued, carried forward by the next generation. Daniel passed away, leaving behind a legacy of steadiness and care.

Lucy Jane (1835–1849) lived for 14 years. A young woman with a promising spiritual life was cut short, but never forgotten, as her legacy lingers within her family.

Lydia Louisa (1837–1883) lived for 46 years, a life shaped by family and devotion. Lydia married Christopher Martin Brazee, and together they had two children: Catherine Lilian and Martin Holmes. Despite having fewer years than some of her siblings, Lydia's legacy remains through her children and reminiscences in the Holmes family history.

# Echoes: Family Reflections

*Behind every landmark and law was a family, bound by blood, love, or necessity, whose stories deserve to be told. Genealogical sketches, emotional truths, and the threads that bind generations.*

## *Family Reflections*

Land as far as the eye can see,
settlers looking for the perfect home,
faith and belief in a good life to come.
Congregating, connections of faith, morals
sustainability, a future of generations
Love, loss and loyalty, the bonds of the family.
The perfections with flaws,
the pain, grief, hardships, unforeseen
What's to come?
Remembrances, tributes to previous generations
Carrying on traditions,
making new traditions,
blending in the community
Contributing to the family
Contributing to the community,
holding hands at prayer
A time for laughter,
a time for reflection,
every moment in time,
cherished.
– *Amy Shannon 2025*

# The Balls

The Ball family originated Balls-Town, a community shaped by faith, generosity, and reserved leadership. Reverend Eliphalet Ball led his congregation to settle on land he had purchased, guiding them not only in spirit but in practical care. He inspired his community to contribute labor and supplies to build a church that still stands today. Though fire consumed much of the building in the 1990s, the original steeple survived, a lasting symbol of resilience and devotion, much like the family who first raised it.

Reverend Eliphalet (1722-1797) was a man of intense faith. He was loyal, a patriot, a reverend, a father and founder of Balls-Town, creating an entire community. Eliphalet was born in New Haven, CT.

 He was the son of John Ball and Mary Tuttle. He had four siblings, John, Mary, Timothy and Stephen. In 1770, Reverend Ball moved from his hometown of Bedford, NY, and settled on a farm. It became the farm of Colonel Samuel Young, a farmer who was a lawyer and politician. The settlement of his was set up beyond the old "Academy Hill."

Reverend Ball married Elizabeth Flamen Ball, and together they had five children. Eliphalet kept the naming tradition of his family when naming their children. Elizabeth, named after her mother, died at 15. Cornelius died when he was about 21 years old. Mary grew up and married James Gordon. John, Flamen, and Stephen served in the Revolutionary War. John, Mary, Flamen, and Stephen traveled with their father and mother to their new home in 1770, which became Balls-Town.

Elizabeth Flamen Ball passed away in 1782, while traveling between Balls-Town and New Haven, CT.

Reverend Ball married Ruth Beecher in 1783. She was the daughter of Joseph Beecher and Elizabeth Alling. Ruth and Reverend Ball did not have any children together, but Ruth had a daughter. Ruth Beecher died in 1804 and is buried at Briggs Cemetery.

When Reverend Ball got there and Balls-Town was acquired, the settler population grew. Certain immigrants came from Ireland, Scotland, while others were simply heading north from the New England states, including New Jersey, to locate a spot to settle. Many of the early settlers would do trades with the Native Americans, especially in the Mohawk Valley area in Schenectady. Schenectady existed as a locale where many transactions and acquisitions would occur.

Reverend Eliphalet Ball's remains rest in Briggs Cemetery. He was honored with a grand stone, with the inscription, "*Sic transit, gloria mundi.* (So, the Glory to the World). Sacred to the memory of Rev. Eliphalet Ball, who died April 6, 1797. Depart, my friends; dry your tears. I must lie here 'til Christ appears."

Mary (1753-1803) was a devoted member of the church and a huge supporter of her father's. She shared the same faith and endurance as her father. (See The Gordons)

Colonel John Ball (1756-1838) got a commission in Colonel Wynkoop's Regiment during the Revolutionary War. At the time that he was a lieutenant, he marched to Fort Stanwix, and helped cause the end of British control, and he overcame General John Burgoyne. He rose to the rank of colonel of militia. John survived and became the first supervisor of Milton and represented Saratoga County in the state assembly.

John enjoyed sharing stories about his father with people who showed interest. At one point, he was quoted saying to Theodore Dwight, who had visited John, "At the time of my father's first coming to Ballston, the low grounds near the Springs were covered with a forest, and the old Spring, the only one then known -was overflown by the brook when it was much swollen by the rain."

Many of the parishioners from Bedford and Stamford in Connecticut joined Ball and settled in parts of the land within the five-mile tract. One of Reverend Ball's congregates, Epenetus White, who was a senator at Stamford, his family settled on Long Lake (now, it is referred to as Ballston Lake). After there was word that there were settlement homesteads, other families arrived and settled. By 1772, twenty families were settled. Reverend Ball's leadership and God-fearing beliefs made it so that he was wise to create a foundation for a new community. He did his best to keep his morals and virtues to lead his congregation. John died in but left a legacy of faith and loyalty.

Captain Stephen Ball (1759-1800), a soldier during the Revolutionary War, served in Colonel Wynkoop's Regiment. After the war, he became one of the first five coroners of the country in 1796-1797. Stephen was a loyal soldier and son.

Stephen held the position of captain and leader of the Militia of Balls-Town Fort. He received notice from Colonel James Gordon, advising the forces at the fort of Munroe's inhuman order and requesting that no attempt be made to rescue the prisoners. However, Captain Ball had already started the process of prisoner releases and trades. This unfortunately ended up with the "Burning of Balls-Town" and the British soldiers, Tories, and their allies, the Iroquois Native Americans, taking bloody action against the settlers, including the kidnapping and murder of several men.

He often worked beside his father, and he had a reputation for teasing or playing pranks on his father, as well as his siblings.

Stephen once said to a couple Reverend Ball was joining in matrimony, and that he was helping his father with, that he anticipated them to kiss repeatedly during the service, which certainly wasn't true, but they did it regardless, and Reverend Ball stated he would leave them half-wed, and the groom, simply said, "Stephen instructed me to." Stephen had not only played a trick on them, but on his father as well.

Stephen Ball married Mary Foster around 1778. Together, they had seven children: Stephen, Mary, Eliphalet, Charlotte, Peter, (infant daughter), and (infant son). Stephen's wife, Mary, died in 1843.

Private Flamen Ball (1761–1816) grew up and joined the service, becoming a private in the Revolutionary War. He then graduated with merit from Yale in 1787 and became a very prominent lawyer in New York City. Flamen married Ann Western, and they had five children. Their children include Ann [1], Ann [2], Flamen Ball II, Elizabeth , and Emily. Flamen was buried at Trinity Church, New York City.

# The Booths

*Before diving into the lives of this Booth family, I wish to give a huge thank you to Susan Strange, a descendant of the Booths, who helped me fill in the gaps, and provide new information. I sent a copy of my work about her family to her, and she replied in kind.*

Ingrained in Ballston Spa, the Lebbeus Booth family carried a legacy of scholarship, civic service, and hushed strength. Lucretia and Lebbeus Booth raised children who spearheaded education, including the advancement of academic rights for women, a cause reflected in both their lives and losses. Their descendants continued this legacy, honoring those who passed too soon while carrying forward the Booth name through public service, teaching, and reminiscence. The family's story is one of intellect and endurance, woven through generations with grace.

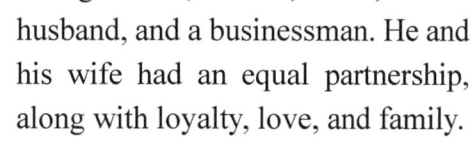

Lebbeus (1784-1859) was a lifelong learner, teacher, father, dutiful

husband, and a businessman. He and his wife had an equal partnership, along with loyalty, love, and family.

Lebbeus' was born in Stratford, Connecticut to Nathaniel Booth and Martha Hinman.

In 1821, Lebbeus married Lucretia Foot, a union that would become a cornerstone of educational reform and community uplift in Ballston Spa. Three years later, they co-founded the *Ballston Spa Female Seminary,* a bold endeavor when women's education was still considered ornamental. Lucretia served as principal, shaping curriculum and character, while Lebbeus conducted operations and outreach. They had distinct roles but were intricately linked, a model of mutual respect and shared mission.

But their partnership didn't end at the schoolhouse door. As Lebbeus served as village trustee, bank director, and superintendent of the poor, it was likely Lucretia's insights, shaped by her work with young women, informed his decisions. Her experience with education and moral development may have influenced his leadership in the Bible Society and Christ Church vestry. After the seminary closed, Lebbeus turned to manufacturing and finance. Even if records don't mention Lucretia in these positions, her organizational ability and community links show she had more than a quiet role.

Together, they raised children who mirrored their values, lawyers, legislators, and educators. Their sons' achievements in law and public service reflect the intellectual rigor and civic spirit nurtured at home.

Their partnership was not performative; it was purposeful. Lucretia wasn't simply "the wife of Lebbeus Booth" or "Mrs. Lebbeus Booth." She was a leader, a parent, a moral guide, and a strategist behind the scenes in his public life.

Lucretia took part in societal events. In fact, one news article stated that "Mrs. Lebbeus Booth" is one of the judges of needlework contests at the county fair.

Lebbeus died in 1859, and he is buried in the family plot, alongside his wife, in the Ballston Spa Village Cemetery.

At Ballston, Dec. 16, LEBBEUS BOOTH, Esq., aged about 70 years. Mr. Booth was a graduate of Union College, and educated for the ministry at Princeton; but his health failing, he did not complete his theological studies and turned his attention to the higher branches of teaching. He was the second Principal of the Albany female Academy for several years. In 1824 he established at Ballston a Seminary for young ladies, which he conducted with eminent success for many years, and where a large number of the most intelligent ladies, now in middle life, were educated. Mr. Booth was a well educa'ed, upright, high-minded and honorable man. He commanded the universal respect of the community in which he lived, and exemplified in his life and deportment all the virtues of the true and devout Christian.

BOOTH—At her residence in Ballston Spa, Oct. 31, Lucretia Booth, widow of the late Lebeus Booth, in the 68th year of her age.

Together, they had 12 children; a few of the children died incredibly young. Lebbeus and Lucretia raised an accomplished family, as faith, confidence, love, loyalty, and higher education were the base of their family.

Elizabeth (1822–1838) died at 15 years-6 months of "the consumption" (tuberculosis). The loss was a deep one to the family, but Elizabeth's memory always lived on, even if her life was cut short. She was probably emulating her mother and looking forward to a grand academic future.

John [1] (1824–1830) died at 6 of "the canker sore throat." His running footsteps, simple giggles and laughs, still echoed when he was gone. His dinner chair was empty but honored.

Martha [1] (1826–1827) died at 3 months, because "of the croup", leaving an empty cradle, but never being forgotten. She was honored by her sister, carrying her name, and living a fruitful and faithful life.

Martha [2] (1830–1912) was honored in carrying on her older sister's life, even though she never met her. Martha married Lindsley Seelye in 1852. Lindsley passed away in 1868 at 39, leaving Martha a young widow with two daughters, Caroline and Sarah "Bessie."
Caroline married William Hubert Burr, and they had two sons and one daughter: Marion Elizabeth (1881-1968), William Fairfield (1884–1908), and George Lindsley (1889–1971). Caroline's lifespan remained short; she passed away at 40, but her impact lived on thanks to her offspring.
Bessie Seelye Arnold (1854-1932) was widowed twice and did not have any children.

John [2] (1832-1862) was honored in being named after his older brother, one he had never met, as his life was cut short. Before reaching the age of twenty, John established a private school in Craneville, just two miles north of the village of Ballston Spa. He served as proof of his initial devotion to education and guidance. He later pursued law under the guidance of Judge George Scott, completing his clerkship and passing the bar in 1853. John quickly gained recognition as a successful attorney, known not only for his legal acumen but also for his eloquence and love of literature and poetry. People admired his public speaking for its grace and force.

*John Chester Booth*

John began compiling a history of Saratoga County, a labor of intellect and heart that he completed two years before his death. Grose added it to the *Centennial History of the Village of Ballston Spa*, preserving John's voice for future generations. Unfortunately, John didn't live to see his work published.

He died in 1860 at just 28 years old, his lifelong frailty finally overtaking him. One can only wonder what literary brilliance the world lost with his passing. John had two daughters: Ella "Cuddy" (see Women of Worth) and Martha "Mattie," who died in her sleep from diphtheria at 7 years old.

Mary [1] (1833–1835) died at 1 year, of the "croup and scarlet fever." She was just shy of taking her first steps or uttering her first words, but her laughter and crying stole the hearts of her family.

Moss (1832–1853) was selected as a Commencement Orator at Union College in 1847, a sign of his intellect and promise. He served as principal of the public school in Southington, Connecticut, before studying law under Judge Hammond in Ballston Spa. Moss practiced law in Boston, Massachusetts, and served as a member of the Massachusetts Legislature. He later returned to Ballston Spa, where his life was cut short in 1853 at thirty. Though brief, his journey reflected a deep commitment to education, public service, and the law.

Mary [2] (1835–1836) died at 1 year. Another loss for the Booth family, losing another Mary, who held her older sister's name, but left as quickly as Mary did before her.

Isabella (1839–1856) entered Troy Female Seminary in 1854, preparing to graduate with the class of 1856. Her future held promise, shaped by learning and hushed determination. Tragically, Isabella died at seventeen, taken by a contagious fever that swept through the region during that time. Her obituary stated she died of typhoid fever, and "lingered four weeks and has finally succumbed to the power of the disease." Her life, though brief, reflected the grace and potential of a young woman devoted to education and growth.

Lucretia (1840–1927) was named after her mother. Lucretia carried forward both a name and a legacy of hushed strength. She married the Reverend George Washington Dean, S.T.D., and together they had three sons: Keble, Philip Sidney and Bernard Kent.

Reverend Dean served as rector of Christ Church in Ballston Spa for six years before accepting a professorship in Latin at Racine College in Wisconsin. After eight years there, he returned east to become rector of St. Stephen's Church in Schuylerville, a position he held until his death in 1880.

Lucretia lived to the age of 86, passing away from pneumonia. Her long-life bridged eras of faith, family, and devotion, her name a living thread between generations.

*Susan Edwards*

Josiah (1842–1843) died at 8 months, leaving behind his empty cradle and his mother's open arms.

Susan (1843–1916) married Moses Mason Robinson in 1877. Together, they had two daughters: Lucretia Booth Robinson Evans and Ethel Mason Robinson Arnold Strange. Through them, Susan's name and the Booth legacy continued into the next generation, woven into both family and community life. Lucretia Booth Robinson Evans had three children, and then that bloodline ended, since she had no grandchildren. However, Ethel Mason Robinson married Edwin Bruton Strange in 1910. They had four children, Edwin Bruton Strange III, Theodore Booth Strange, Hinman Foot Strange and Susan Booth Strange. All four married and have living descendants as of this printing.

*(Left to Right) Susan Edwards (Booth) Robinson; Martha (Booth) Seelye (1830-1912) in mourning dress; and Lucretia (Booth) Dean*

**Special thanks to Susan Strange, a descendant of the Booth family (by Susan Edwards), for the photos.**

# Lebbeus Booth's Life in the News

Correspondence between the Whig Congressional Convention, for the 16th District, and A. L. Linn.

BALLSTON SPA, OCT. 1, 1842.

Hon. A. L. LINN—

The Whig Congressional Convention, for the XVIth District, held this day at Galway Corners, unanimously nominated you as the Candidate to represent said District in the twenty-eighth Congress: And a resolution was passed directing the Chairman of the Convention to inform you of your nomination, and request your acceptance of the same.

Your ob't. serv't.

LEBBEUS BOOTH, Chairman.

BALLSTON SPA BANK.—The following gentlemen were on Tuesday last, elected Directors:

James M. Cook, James Thompson, Eli Barnum Lebbeus Booth, John W. Thompson, Isaac Frink Harvey Chapman, Anson Brown, Samuel Hides Stephen Smith, Rockwell Putnam, Robert Speir Jonathan S. Beach.

At a subsequent meeting of the Board, JAMES M. COOK, was unanimously elected President, and LEBBEUS BOOTH, Vice-President, for the ensuing year.

TEMPERANCE MEETING.—At the annual meeting of the Saratoga County Temperance Society, held at the Baptist church in this village on the 7th ult. the following officers were elected for the ensuing year: Hon. E. Cowen, President. J. Knickerbacker, J. Gilchrist, and S. Freeman, Vice Presidents. Anson Brown, Cor. Sec'ry. Lebbeus Booth, Rec. Sec'ry. L. Booth, A. Brown, H. Gardner, E. H. Kimball, and W. G. Verplanck, Ex. Com.

The following resolutions were passed:

Resolved, That all the local Temperance Societies in this county be requested to hold meetings on 25th February next—the day appointed by the American Temperance Society for simultaneous meetings.

Resolved, That the several local societies in the county be requested to prepare and forward their annual reports to Anson Brown, or L. Booth, in the village of Ballston Spa, on or before the first Wednesday of March next.

Resolved, That the traffic in *ardent spirits*, as a drink, is an immorality; and ought to be abandoned throughout the world.

Resolved, That those members of Temperance societies, who furnish grain or other articles for distillation, act inconsistently with their *pledge*.

Elder S. S. Parr then delivered an address appropriate to the occasion.

On motion of H. Gardner, Esqr. the thanks of the Society were presented to Elder Parr, for his able address.

The Society then adjourned to meet at the Episcopal church in the village of Ballston Spa, on the first Tuesday of January 1835.

The Booth Family Final Resting Place

# The Curtisses/Curtis

The Curtiss family, with roots in England and early Connecticut, embodied the reticent strength of American pioneers. Their name may have changed over time, but their commitment to building, both land and legacy, remained constant. **(An incredibly special thank you for family information to William Curtiss of Ballston Spa. He was nice enough to share his family tree with me.)**

Jonathan Curtiss (1710-1768) married Eunice Hawley (1720-1796), daughter of Henry Hawley and Mary Pickett, in 1735. They lived in Connecticut. They had five children.

Mary (1748-1790) married Ephraim Judson (1739-1813).

Timothy (1749-1812) lived in Stratford, Connecticut.

Sarah (1751-1801) moved to Charlton and then married Gideon Hawley (1744-1840) in 1770.

Jonathan (1754-1818) moved to Ballston and lived in the area until he passed away.

Andrew (1756-1840) was born in Huntington, Connecticut. Andrew came from a family whose name carried many spellings—Curtice, Curtiss, and Curtis. Some of the family members spelled it with a single 's' and others continued to use the double 'ss' at the end of their name, even descendants that are still living in Ballston Spa.

Andrew married Patience Nichols, daughter of Nathan Nichols and Elizabeth Trowbridge, in 1779, and together they had one son, Elisha. Andrew served as a soldier in the Revolutionary War, stationed in New York during its occupation by the British. After the war, he settled in Charlton for nine years before purchasing a farm in Ballston.

Andrew and Patience are buried in Briggs Cemetery, their lives grounded in early American resilience and unassuming devotion. Andrew and Patience's legacies live on through their descendants, and some of those people still live in the Ballston Spa area. They had two children, Betsey and Eunice.

Elizabeth "Betsey" (1781-1850) moved to Charlton. She married Silas Sherman (1772-1849) in 1793.

Eunice (1785-1855) married Edward Taylor, son of John and Chloë Taylor, in 1807. (See the Taylor family.)

John Orville (1807-1886) married Ann (1817-1891). They had three children, Matthew, George, and William.

Ann Maria (1809-1886) married Solomon Waring. Their children were Richard Solomon, Orville Taylor, Ann, Sarah [1], Malvina, Edward, Marietta, Luzerne, Phebe, Elisha, William, Jane, Eunice (who married Alexander Hubbs), Sarah [2], and Susan Patience.

Abijah Nichols (1791-1865) married Naomi Smith (1788-1848), daughter of Jesse Smith Jr. and Phoebe Kellogg, in 1813. He married Eunice Barrus (1802-1886) in 1849.

William (1814-1892), son of Abijah and Naomi, married Martha Vanostrand (1820-1862). He married Amanda McBride (1815-1884). He married Phebe (1817-1844). William was a justice of the peace. William and Martha's children were, Frances, Anna Naomi, and Anson (who married Esther Maria Smith, daughter of John Platt Smith and Agnes Eusebia Northrup, in 1879), Angeline, (who married Franklin McLean in 1873) and Martha "Mattie" (who married James Thompson in 1884).

Edward and Eunice had children, where there isn't much of a record of anything about their lives, but their lives matter, whether or not documented. Rosetta, Andrew, Charlotte, Anson and Asa.

Elisha (1793-1881) lived with his father until the age of 23, beginning his life as a farmer before stepping into a broader legacy of infrastructure and innovation. He married Elizabeth Waterman in 1815, and after her passing, married her sister Belinda in 1909. Elisha and Elizabeth had three children.

Elisha became an assistant to Colonel Samuel Young, Erie Canal Commissioner, and worked on the canal's construction until its completion in 1825. He then became superintendent, a role he kept until quitting in 1909. In 1829, he purchased the farm adjoining his father's homestead and made substantial improvements. His skill in construction led him to assist in building many of the nation's highways and railroads, including the Albany and Schenectady Railroad, the first in America, and later the Troy and Ballston lines.

Elisha Curtiss

Elisha, Elizabeth, and Belinda are buried in Hillside Cemetery in Burnt Hills. Life included smarts, skill, and a deep calm coming from belief: "Calm came from a constant faith in the One who does everything right, await with composure the final moment that comes to all living." Elisha and Elizabeth had five children.

Asa Waterman (1816-1884) married Ann Caroline Raymond (1817-1855) in 1840. They had two children. Asa inherited the family farm. Asa, a farmer, lived about a half mile south of Ballston Center. "Though nearing three score and ten, he has always enjoyed the best of health". (Note: A "score" is an old-fashioned term for the number twenty. Thus, he died near age seventy. Three score is 60, and "ten" equals 70).

Asa had four marriages, Ann being the initial spouse, and the mother of his kids. He married Sarah in 1856. He married Charlotte in 1858, and married Sarah Palmer in 1869.

In 1884, after Asa finished his task of milking, he went into his house and set down his pails. He complained of pain and died within ten minutes.

Reverend Augustus (1845-1905) was born in Ballston Spa, but he moved to Michigan, where he met and married Eleanor Kent (1851-1895) in 1873. Their only child was Caroline. Elisha was a reverend of a Presbyterian Church.

Nathan (1848-1917), a farmer, wed Julia Miller in 1874. Nathan and Julia didn't have children of their own, but they took in and raised Julia's sister, Adelaide's, son, Raymond Curtis Schutt, when

Adelaide died in 1892.

Frederick (1819–1889) was a Justice of the Peace. He married Mary Elizabeth Dunham (1822-1868). He married Harriet Dunham (1839-1915). He fathered five children with Harriet. Charles, Maddie, Harriet, George, and Libbie.

Elizabeth Abigail (1823–1895) married Asa Hollister (1809-1887). Together, they had two children. Angie (1858-1859) lived just over a year, and Zilpha (1861-1865) lived just over four years.

Luzon (1795-1863) married an unknown spouse in 1830.

Andrew Jr (1798-1822) married Pauline Lyon (1801-1890). They had one child, Alfred (1821-1911).

*Elizabeth Abigail*

Sarah (1800-1879) a lone daughter, sister, though records dismiss her, her family tree did not. She left only a remnant, but still a legacy and a life worth living, and worth remembering.

# The Doubledays

The Doubledays were a family shaped by duty, military service, political engagement, and unshakable faith. Across generations, they served their country both in uniform and in spirit, with soldiers on the battlefield and wives who supported the cause with strength and devotion. Their lives reflected a deep loyalty to country and community, grounded in conviction and guided by belief. In war and peace, the Doubledays stood firm, faithful, patriotic, and resolute.

Ulysses Freeman Doubleday's parents were Abner Doubleday (1757–1812) and Mercy Freeman Doubleday (1762–1817).

*Ulysses Freeman Doubleday*

Ulysses married Hester, whose parents were Thomas D Donnelly (1764–1835) and Ruth Pettinger (1768–1838). They had six children: Thomas, Ruth Marie, Abner, Amanda, Ulysses, and Jane Ann.

With the support of his wife, Hester, Ulysses established and edited the papers, *the Saratoga Courier, the Cayuga Patriot*, and *the Gospel Advocate*. In 1831, he gained election as a Jacksonian to the Twenty-second Congress, serving until 1833. After his term ended, he got the job of inspector of Auburn Prison in 1834 and won the election for the Twenty-fourth Congress, acting 1835-37. Once he departed from politics, he took up agricultural work in Scipio, NY, and later relocated to New York City, where he worked in the commercial sector till his retirement in 1860.

Hester predeceased her husband, as she died at 61 in 1859. She is buried next to her husband. Ulysses died at 73. He is buried at Evergreen Memorial Cemetery in Illinois.

Colonel Thomas Donnelly Doubleday (1816–1864), a man of reserved strength and civic devotion, came from a noteworthy family, their history connecting generations.

Thomas's input was of equal significance to his younger brother, Abner. He married Mary Ward in 1841, and together they raised two children, Mary and Stephen Ward. Their son Stephen

*Thomas Donnelly Doubleday*

would later serve as a lieutenant in Thomas's regiment, wounded in the line of duty, a testament to the family's shared commitment to the Union cause.

Prior to the war, Thomas, a respected bookseller, had a well-known shop on Wall Street in New York City. His desire for education went further than business. When the Civil War erupted, Thomas answered the call not with fanfare but with resolve, organizing and commanding the 4th New York Heavy Artillery to defend Washington, D.C. His leadership helped strengthen the capital during its most susceptible years, and though he resigned his commission in 1863, his service laid a foundation for others to follow. Sadly, his time ended in 1864 after he got hit by a horse-pulled carriage. He rests in Staten Island Cemetery, largely unsung but deeply worthy of reminiscence, not only as a colonel and cultural advocate, but as a husband, father, and brother whose legacy deserves to stand beside those more widely known.

Mary (1818–1882) and Thomas were married in 1841. She built her life alongside Thomas in New York City. Being a mother, she raised her children through unsure times, particularly when Stephen went into his father's group and got injured during a fight. At home, Mary managed the household and supported the family business during Thomas's absence, balancing the reticent strength of a Civil War wife with the emotional weight of watching both husband and son go to war. Even if history mentions her name in passing, her impact must have been clear in each letter, every prayer, and every act of perseverance that kept the family together during hardship.

Second Lieutenant Stephen Ward Doubleday (1845–1926) came into the world in New York City and got his name from a Revolutionary War patriot. Stephen carried forward the family custom of service when, at just seventeen, he enlisted in the Union Army during the Civil War. Serving as a second lieutenant in the very regiment his father captained, he sustained an injury in action as an indication of bravery and family dedication. After the war, Stephen built a distinguished career in finance, becoming a senior partner in several firms and serving as governor of the New York Stock Exchange. He married Angelica Barraclough Cushman in 1875 and raised three children, balancing civic leadership with family life. A lover of golf and travel, he spent years abroad in Berlin and Monaco before returning to NY, where he passed away. His life bridged war and peace, duty and refinement, a quiet echo of his father's legacy, carried forward with grace.

Mary (1842–1912) remains a gentler thread in the family's tapestry. Though historical records speak little of her public life, her presence within the Doubleday household would have been shaped by the same currents of war, resilience, and cultural endeavor that defined her family. As her father led troops and her brother served in battle, Mary held the home together, offering steadiness in a time of uncertainty. Regardless of communication, support, or peaceful company, her function held the same importance. In a family of soldiers and scholars, Mary's life reminds us that history is held in the hands of those who wait, who listen, and who remember. Her legacy, though softly spoken, belongs in the chorus of reminiscence.

Ruth (1817–1888) married Dudley P G Everts in 1835. Their children were Miriam, Hester, Ulysses (named after Ruth's brother), Jane (named after Ruth's late sister), María and Ruth (named after her mother).

Major General Abner Doubleday (1819-1893) was a Civil War Union Major General. He graduated from the America Military Academy at West Point. Abner entered the service as a cadet and worked his way up to major general in the Union Army during the Civil War.

On the first day of the Battle of Gettysburg, he began the day as the senior division commander in the Army of the Potomac's I Corps. When the Commander Major General got killed in the beginning of the battle, General Doubleday assumed leadership of the soldiers on the field and defended the Federal left side during much of the rest of the day's struggle. Even though his troops eventually fell back to Cemetery Hill in retreat, he stopped the Confederates for a duration of time so that large parts of the Union Army could get to the site of the fighting and start sturdy defensive positions. Despite his actions under extreme conditions, he was not given credit for his defense and was replaced as Corps Commander.

The plaque on the back of his tombstone reads:
*HE WAS GRADUATED AT WEST POINT 1842*
*1846 MEXICAN WAR*
*1852 COMMISSIONER TO MEXICO*
*1854 INDIAN HOSTILITIES IN TEXAS*
*1856 INDIAN HOSTILITIES IN FLORIDA*
*1861-1865 WAR OF THE REBELLION*
*FORT SUMTER*
*GROVETON SECOND BULL RUN*
*SOUTH MOUNTAIN ANTIETAM*
*FREDERICKSBURG CHANCELLORSVILLE*
*GETTYSBURG*
*1863 TO 1865 PRESIDENT OF MILITARY COMMISSIONS*
*IN CONTINUOUS COMMAND UNTIL RETIRED*

Abner married Mary Hewitt (1823-1907) in 1852. He spoke out against slavery. Abner Doubleday, his father's father, took part in the American Revolution, and Thomas Donnelly, his mother's father, served as a mounted messenger for General Washington. While stationed in San Francisco, he got a patent for the cable car railway, but upon reassignment, he signed away the rights to the patent. Abner died of heart disease and is buried in Arlington National Cemetery. He has had many honors and namesakes, including a statue of him at Gettysburg, and a landmark — his house of his birth, in Ballston Spa, on Washington Street.

Amanda (1823–1892) married the Reverend Herman James Eddy in 1842. They had six children, and they believed in honoring their previous generations. Their children are Adelbert, Herman Jr., Ulysses, William, Thomas, and Lillian.

General Ulysses Doubleday (1824–1893) was a Civil War Union Brevet Brigadier General. He volunteered at the very beginning of the war and served in several commands. First assigned in 1862 as major of the 4th New York Volunteers Heavy Artillery, he got the job to serve on the staff

of his older brother, Abner. In 1863, he gained a commission as lieutenant colonel of the 3rd America Colored Infantry, serving with them for a year until he got promoted to colonel and commander of the 45th America Colored Troops in 1864. He earned the rank of Brevetted Brigadier General in 1865, for "meritorious service" and received an honorable discharge after four years of duty in 1865. After the war, he became a successful stockbroker in New York City. He had two wives, Mary Stewart, whom he married in 1850, and later he married Mary O'Gorman.

*Ulysses Doubleday*

Jane Ann (1830–1843) died at 13. She entered teenager hood, but her life was cut short, but her laughter, her ability to make her family smile, and her promising future, never faltered.

# The Dunnings

John Dunning (1681–1734) married Sarah Lambert (1689–1760). John's parents were Benjamin and Mary Dunning. Sarah's parents were Jesse and Deborah Lambert. John and Sara had eight children, and their generations grew with grandchildren, and their children, and so on.

Samuel (1712–1735) was remembered as a son and a brother. His story is silent in the record, yet his presence endures.

John (1713–1794) married Hannah Keeler. With their six children, his eighty-one years remain part of the family's enduring story.

Richard (1713–1797) had a close-knit relationship with his twin brother, John. He was a husband and son. His life with Abigail Betts is carried forward in family reminiscences.

Deacon Matthew Sr. (1719–1807) life spanned nearly nine decades. His first wife was Abigail Patchen, and his second wife was Mary. His presence endures in the family legacy.

David (1722–1777) married Hannah Mead in 1746. His fifty-five years are remembered in family and legacy.

Sarah (1724–1753) named after her mother, married Joseph Hudson. She lived twenty-nine years, her story woven into the family tapestry. A young woman with her life in front of her, cut short leaving behind a mourning husband, and an empty rocking chair.

Hannah (1721-1805) married Aaron Gregory. Her endurance and love brought life to everyone she was around. Her 84 years suggest a strong woman with a zest for life and family.

Michael (1726-1813) had two wives named Hannah. He also had a farm in Malta, *The Dunning Farm*. Michael married Hannah Green (1723–1775). Her grave is the oldest gravesite in Dunning Street Rural Cemetery. It was offset from Dunning Farm, where it started as a family cemetery.

Hannah Green, the first Mrs. Dunning, and Michael had six children: Hannah, Tammissin, Michael Jr, Mary, Ebenezer and Richard.

Hannah Morehouse (1740–1815) the second Mrs. Dunning, was the widow of Edmond Rowland. She and Michael didn't have children. Michael is buried between the graves of his two wives in the Dunning Cemetery. In 1837, the family cemetery became a public cemetery. Currently, the cemetery is located on Dunning Street, aptly named after the Dunnings.

The Dunning Family's Final Resting Place

# The Ellsworths

George Ellsworth (1758–1840) married Sarah Reynolds. Together, they had 12 children. He once said he didn't know his birth date but believed the year to be 1758 because his parents told him so. He served for 8 months and 27 days in the NYS Militia in service to America. The Militia was commanded by Capt. Joshua Taylor, and served in the 12th Regt. commanded by Col. Jacobus Van Schoonhoven. George served as a soldier, taking part in the battle of Bemus Heights, and was present at the surrender of Burgoyne. Sarah and George were married in 1786.

Benjamin (1788–1869) married Roxanna Packard, and they had one son, Lorenzo. Benjamin later married Sarah Jane Taft, and together they had six children: Lucy, Dillie Belle, Minnie Dean, Frank, Fred, and Ida.

Phoebe's (1789–) life traced only in beginnings, yet she remains part of the family's legacy.

Peggy (1792–1888), remembered as a daughter, sister, and wife. She married into the Miller family, her ninety-six years a testament to endurance.

Eliza (1794–1888) is remembered as daughter, sister, and wife. She wed Mr. Graham, and her life spanned nearly a century.

William (1798–) married Huldah. His life is marked in beginnings and kinship, though the record leaves his end untold.

Violetta (1803–1890) married Clemmons Gibbs (1797–1873). Together, they had three children: Catherine, Electa Matilda, and James.

Mary (1804–1879) married David West. Together, they had four children: Eliza Ruth, Henry, Myron, and Helen.

Angeline (1807–) wed Mr. Magill. As mother to Charles, Albert, and Francis, her life is traced in family, though history leaves her end untold.

Horace (1808–1876) married Susan (1812-1890). They raised five children: Daniel, Maria, Angeline, Henry, and Ellen.

Colonel Ephraim Ellsworth (1809–1889) learned the tailor's trade before his 19th birthday and afterwards worked at it in Troy and Jonesville. In 1836,  he married Phebe Denton of Malta, and then moved to Mechanicville to continue his trade, living there the rest of his days, except for the ten years spent in the government's service. In November 1861, President Lincoln commissioned him a captain in the ordnance department, and he was assigned to duty at Fortress Monroe. Captain Ellsworth soon resigned and was placed in charge of the Champlain arsenal, where he remained for about ten years. He returned to his in Mechanicville in the fall of 1871. The couple had two children.

Colonel Elmer Ellsworth (1837-1861) was a military leader, who is still remembered today, but not everyone knows why he has a landmark in Malta, New York. He was born in Mechanicville, NY, and spent part of his youth in New York City before heading westward. In 1854, he settled in Rockford, Illinois, where he worked for a patent agency and began studying military science in his spare hours. By 1857, he had become drillmaster of the local militia, the Rockford Greys, and soon extended his training efforts to units in Milwaukee and Madison, Wisconsin.

Inspired by the fierce discipline and striking appearance of the French Zouave troops in Algeria, he adopted their style and methods. His men wore grand, theatrical uniforms and drilled with precision,

transforming into a nationally prominent exhibition team. In 1859, he moved to Chicago to study law, working as a clerk and immersing himself in legal practice. A year later, he joined Abraham Lincoln in Springfield, assisting with the presidential campaign and studying law in Lincoln's office.

When Lincoln won the presidency, he accompanied him to Washington, D.C., in early 1861. As war clouds gathered, he answered the call to serve, raising the 11th New York Volunteer Infantry Regiment, known as the "Fire Zouaves", from the city's volunteer firefighting companies. He returned to Washington as their colonel, ready to defend the Union.

*Colonel Elmer E. Ellsworth*

Across the Potomac River, a defiant Confederate banner flew above the Marshall House Inn in Virginia, making sure its provocation was visible from the capital. On May 24, 1861, Elmer led his troops across the river and into Alexandria, encountering no resistance. After securing key locations, he turned his attention to the banner. Accompanied by seven men, he entered the Marshall House and climbed the stairs to remove the flag.

Flag in hand, as he reached the bottom of the stairs, he was shot in the chest by Jackson, the inn's owner. Jackson was immediately killed by one of the colonel's men. Dying at each other's feet, each man became a symbol for their cause.

The news of his death brought President Lincoln a deep sadness. An honor guard brought his body to the White House, where he lay in state in the East Room. Later, he was taken to New York City's City Hall, where thousands came to pay tribute to the first conspicuous casualty of the American Civil War. Elmer was a young man whose passion, discipline, and loyalty marked him as a soldier of both spirit and conviction.

President Lincoln spoke to Elmer's parents. "In the untimely loss of your noble son, our affliction here is scarcely less than your own. So much promised usefulness to our country, and bright hopes for oneself and friends, have rarely been so suddenly darkened as in his fall. In size, in years, in youthful appearance, a boy only, his power to command men was surprisingly great. This power, combined with fine intellect and indomitable energy, and a taste altogether military, constituted in him, as seemed to me, the best natural talent in that department I ever knew."

On his monument, it states:

*COL ELMER E. ELLSWORTH, COMMANDER OF THE 1st REGIMENT OF NEW YORK FIRE ZOUAVES. BORN AT MALTA. SARATOGA CO. N.Y. APRIL 11. 1837 KILLED AT ALEXANDRIA. VA. MAY 24th, 1861. IN TAKING THE FIRST BATTLE FLAG IN THE WAR FOR THE UNION THE VOLUNTEER FIRE DEPT THE CITY OF NEW YORK COOPERATED IN ERECTING THIS MONUMENT*

Charley (1841–1860) lived but eighteen years. Though smallpox silenced his life, memory keeps him near.

George (1814–1867) lived fifty-three years. He rests at Greenridge Cemetery, Saratoga Springs, remembered as a son and brother.

Judith (1815-1888) married Marshall Pierce. Together, they had four children: Celinda, John, Sarah, and Mary.

# The Gordons

Ingrained in the early fabric of Saratoga County, the Gordon family carried both military distinction and deep local ties. General James Gordon, a noted figure of the Revolutionary War, brought honor to the region through his service and leadership. Mary Ball Gordon, his spouse, the offspring of Eliphalet Ball, after whom Ballston Spa was christened, bringing together two core heritages. Melinda and young Alexander came into a lineage formed by courage, community, and endurance.

General James Gordon (1739-1810) was a patriarch, soldier, father, husband, and community leader.

He was a pioneer whose name is associated with the most stirring events of past times, with the most important civil positions, town, county, State, and national. In the catalogue of public officials, his name repeatedly appears. He was from County Antrim, Ireland, when a boy of seventeen or eighteen; went back, returned, and (after being in the Indian trade at Albany) in the year 1771 or 1772, finally settled in Ballston, and located where Eugene Wiswell once lived.

The Gordon house was a little southwest of the present house. He was actively in service during the Revolutionary war and was promoted through successive grades to the rank of general. He was taken prisoner by the Tories in 1780 and brought to Canada. He was removed from Quebec to the Isle of Orleans, and finding his old neighbors taken in the second raid of 1781, they effected their escape, and, after severe hardships and starvation, they reached Boston grateful to find that peace was declared.

James led the families that made their home on Middleline Road in Balls-Town. Gordon got 1000 acres along Middle Line Road (then known as The Middle-line), where he soon could bring in settlers, and constructed saw and grist mills (which is a mill to create cereal). He became a leader to all.

In October of that year, Munro divided his troops, and they were resolved to attack Ballston, and its prominent leaders of the local Militia. Gordon was attacked in his own home, his wife Mary, next to him, when Munro stopped the Native American who confronted him with a hatchet. The Gordons had several slaves and a large household. Gordon and his farmhands were taken.

The Gordons did their best to preserve their family's legacy. There is a document called the *Reminiscences of James Gordon*. James wrote this document, and it surfaced later, where it was in the possession of Mrs. William Gordon VerPlanck. Her husband was a great-great-grandson of James Gordon.

William VerPlanck, Melinda's eldest son, had the document, and passed it on. There was an original memorandum written by Melinda about her father. James Gordon was also a writer, who found that it came naturally to write his thoughts or even feelings down on paper. His writings add to preserving his legacy, but some only know Gordon as a General, taken from his home during the Revolutionary War, while his wife and child could only hide.

General Gordon's obituary in a local paper stated, "Jany 19, 1810 General James Gordon. "When the Revolutionary war commenced, he took an active and decided part in favor of our Independence. At that trying time, the prowess of a soldier and the prudence of a civilian were united in him. To personal exertions as a partisan and counselor, in common with others, he born the fatigues incident to the revolution and dangers of conflict with surprising fortitude … so worthy a patriot inspired public confidence, which he retained many years after the struggles he had experiences ceased. He was honored with a seat in Congress under the new Constitution and a seat in the Senate of this state, by the free suffrage of the people."

"My flesh shall slumber in the ground, Till the last trumpet's joyful sound; Then burst the chains with sweet surprise, And in my Saviour's image rise."

Gordon visited his homeland, Ireland, and when he returned to America, he bought land in the settlement of Balls-Town and set up mills on the Mourning Kill Creek (Later, part of this creek was named after James Gordon, because of his stature in the community). Gordon's family joined him and purchased land parcels. Gordon married Mary Ball.

A year after Mary died, he wrote to a friend, "I have an affectionate Child with whom I expect to spend the remainder of my days … and I have more than sufficient to render me independent. In the fall of 1809, James returned to Ballston, Staying in the same place where his grandsons were "accommodated" for five dollars a week. He wished to spend the winter with them. In 1810, James passed away at 54. He is buried alongside his wife and son in Briggs Cemetery.

Mary (1753-1803) was a devoted member of the church and ally of her father's. Mary and her daughter, Melinda, along with several servants, survived the *Fire of Balls-Town*, which is when the British and Iroquois banned together, and killed or kidnapped several men during the Revolutionary War. A friend of James, Isaac Stowe, was killed during the raid. Mary took care of her daughter, and kept their household running, and maintained her faith, while she waited for word about her husband. He was held prisoner in Canada, along with friends, and his last slave, but eventually returned when the war ended. Mary supported her husband in all his endeavors, especially when he was making their home into a thriving community. There were rises in land values, old highways being rebuilt or fixed, and adding more roads.

Mary Ball Gordon died at 50.

Melinda Gordon VerPlanck Waller (1779-1857) was the cherished daughter of James and Mary. Melinda married William Beekman VerPlanck, son of Philip VerPlanck and Effie Beekman, in 1798. Together, they had three children: Mary Ann, William Gordon, and Philip.

Melinda Gordon married Henry Waller in 1806, after her first husband's death. Together, they had six children: Elizabeth, Melinda, Elizabeth, Henry, Joseph, William, Mary, and James.

Alexander (1784-1793) experience of life was mild and fleeting, totaling merely nine years. Even though he did not reach maturity, Alexander's memory was treasured. His father, James, was buried close to him, a demonstration of everlasting affection and recollection. Together, their graves mark a hushed corner of family history, where presence and absence are held side by side.

*COMMUNICATION.*

DIED, on the night of the 17th instant, at the house of JOHN GIBSON, Esq. in the 71st year of his age, General JAMES GORDON, long an inhabitant of Ballston.

General Gordon was a native of Ireland, and at an early age came to America. When the revolutionary war commenced, he took an active and decided part in favor of our Independence. At that trying time, the prowess of a soldier and the prudence of a civilian were united in him. To personal exertions as a partizan and a counsellor, in common with others, he bore the fatigues incident to the revolution, and the dangers of conflict, with surprizing fortitude.

In this virtue, none exceeded him. A character so worthy a patriot, inspired public confidence, which he retained many years after the struggles he had experienced, ceased. He was honored with a seat in Congress under the new Constitution, and a seat in the Senate of this state, by the free suffrages of the people.

At all times when society called for his services, his sympathies were awake. If his country required it, he was ready to lend his aid. If the poor were distressed, he generously and without ostentation offered his purse. As a Christian, he was examplary; as a citizen, able in advice and experience; as a man, honest and upright; and as a politician, sage and discreet. He died as he lived, a sincere Christian, and friend to his species—regretted and lamented by his relatives, and all who were acquained with his virtues.

—— In this village, on Saturday morning, SAMUEL M'NEAL, in the 14th year of his age.

# The Groses

## *Henry Lawrence (1816-1898)*

REV. H. L. GROSE.

Henry Lawrence Grose was the beloved son of Henry Gross and Betsey Fabrique, and one of seven siblings. Henry's early education was not from institutions, but from his father. A Columbia College graduate, who nurtured both intellect and purpose.

Henry's path was remarkable. He apprenticed in medicine with doctors in Fort Plain, and by 1836, began his practice in Owego. Yet even as he took care of the body, he was drawn to the printed word. He learned the typographical arts and published a paper in Montgomery County before acquiring the *Ballston Journal* in 1860.

He wrote, edited, and printed until age gently stilled his pen. His sons, H. Seward, Edward, Howard, and Charles, each took turns at the press, the ink of their father's legacy staining their hands. But Henry's

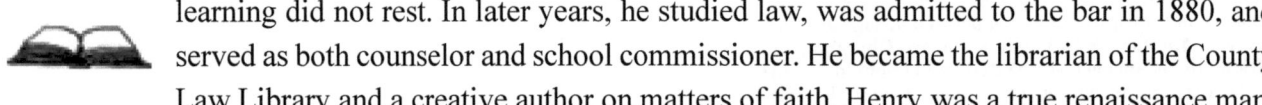

learning did not rest. In later years, he studied law, was admitted to the bar in 1880, and served as both counselor and school commissioner. He became the librarian of the County Law Library and a creative author on matters of faith. Henry was a true renaissance man.

Through it all, he remained a Baptist minister, never retreating, never faltering. Theology, medicine, law, language, and print: Henry Grose lived each vocation as a deepening.

He married Emma Seward in 1840, and Lucy Candee in 1893. His life was not marked by fame, but by fidelity, to learn, to service, and endurance. Reverend Grose was a life-long learner, and Ballston Spa remembers him not only in archives, but in the echo of pages turned, sermons spoken, and sons who carried forward the ink.

Mary (1843–1925) married Justin Smith in 1873. With their son Henry, her eighty-two years remain part of the family's enduring story.

Henry (1845–1904) married Hortense Young. He labored with his father and brothers at the press;

his life was carried forward in reminiscence.

Edward (1847-1922) was the author of the book "Centennial History of the village of Ballston Spa," written in 1907. He married Sarah Lee (1848-1916) in 1868. Edward was on the literary committee when planning the centennial celebration of 1907. He was a member of the Masonic Lodge. Edward was an organist, and he served as one of the post masters. From 1888 to 1902, he was a county clerk. Edward and Sarah had four children, Walter Leland, Anna, Edward Lee, and Bessie.

Jane (1849–1898) lived forty-nine years. Though the archives are silent, memory keeps her near. She was remembered as daughter and sister. Her life is traced only in dates, yet she belongs to the lineage. Her faith in her family never faltered.

Howard (1852-1939) helped his father and brothers with working the presses. He was also a clergyman, like his father, having a true and deep devotion to his faith.

Charles (1855-1946) married Jenna Kathan in 1890. They had two children; Eleanor and Charles Jr. Charles also helped his father and brothers with managing the press.

CHARLES H. GROSE

Emma (1857-1943) married Charles Eede (1846-1913), and they had three children, Arner, Helen, and Mabelle.

Eleanore (1860–1949) married John Weddell (1855–1932) in 1882. Their children were John, Suzanne, Justin, Margaret, Laurens, Joseph, Thomas, and Eleanore (named after her mother).

Frederick's (1867–1874) story is unfinished in the record, yet his place among siblings endures.

The Boston Globe
Sat, May 20, 1939 · Page 2

## Rev. H. B. Grose

WALTHAM, May 20—Funeral services for Rev. Howard Benjamin Grose, 87, a minister for 50 years and editor of Missions, publication of the American Baptist Home Mission Society, for 23 years, will be held tomorrow. Services will be private.

Dr. Grose died last night after a week's illness from pneumonia at a private hospital. He is survived by his wife, the former Caroline Bristol, and two sons, Howard Jr. of Kingston, R. I., and Laurence R. Grose of Kendal Green, Weston.

For more than 50 years Dr. Grose was prominent in journalistic circles of the Baptist Church. Graduating from Rochester University in 1876, he became New York correspondent for the Chicago Tribune for a short time but later joined the staff of the New York Examiner, a Baptist weekly. He was ordained to the Baptist ministry in 1883 and served in Poughkeepsie, N. Y., and Pittsburg until 1890 when he became president of the University of South Dakota for two years. He became professor of history at the newly organized Chicago University.

He became associate editor of the Watchman, Boston publication until 1900, when he became pastor of the First Baptist Church, Jamaica Plain. He resigned in 1903 to become editorial secretary of the American Baptist Home Missions Society and in 1910 he became editor of Missions. He retired in 1933 and was made editor-emeritus for life.

Dr. Grose was born in Millerton, N. Y., the son of a minister, Rev. Henry Laurence Grose.

The Troy Record
Sat, Jan 19, 1946 · Page 9

Charles H. Grose, retired publisher of the oldest newspaper in Saratoga County, the Ballston Journal, died at his residence in Ballston Spa last night following a brief illness. He was ninety years of age. Mr. Grose retired five years ago, turning the weekly publication over to his son, Charles H. Grose, jr.

He was born in Galway in 1855, the son of Rev. Henry L. Grose and Emma Louisa Seward. His father was the Baptist pastor there at the time but Mr. Grose spent practically all his life in Ballston. It was in 1860 that his father purchased the Ballston Journal and the family moved here but during the early sixties the family moved to Hydeville, Vt., where his father was pastor for five years. Since then Ballston has been the home of the family.

Early in life Mr. Grose was interested in the mechanics of the printing trade and owned a small press with which he printed cards for his friends. On returning from Hydeville he became an apprentice in the office and always retained a liking for this branch of the business, working regularly in the office until five years ago.

He saw the Journal develop into a daily in 1891 which continued until 1939 with a weekly edition also until 1913. Since 1939 the Journal has been a weekly.

In 1872 he became associated with his father under the title of Henry L. Grose & Son, he assuming the business management and his father devoting his time to editorial work and occasionally supplying vicinity pulpits. On the death of the elder Mr. Grose in 1913, he became full owner of the business, and was manager and publisher, but employed others on the editorial work of the newspaper.

### Remained Sole Owner.

He remained sole owner of the business until 1922 when his son, Charles H. Grose, jr., entered the business and was taken in as partner in 1924 under the title of C. H. Grose & Son, and has remained so to the present time. Advancing years, however, found him relinquishing more and more of the business to his son and for the past five years he has acted only in an advisory capacity.

His father being a Baptist min-
(Continued on Page Eleven.)

C. H. GROSE

The Times Record
Sat, Jan 23, 1943 ·Page 2

## Mrs. Emma A. G. Eede.

Mrs. Emma A. Grose Eede, widow of Rev. Charles W. Eede, died at her home in Ballston Spa yesterday after a short illness. Born in Galaway on Sept. 1, 1857, she was the daughter of the late Rev. Henry L Grose, pastor of the Galaway Baptist Church, and Emma Louise Seward, cousin of William A. Seward, member of Abraham Lincoln's cabinet. She was married more than fifty years ago and for a short time lived in the West, before settling in Ballston Spa, where she has resided many years,

A member of the Ballston Spa Baptist Church for 54 years, she is survived by three daughters, Mrs. Russell McQuay of Emporium, Pa.; Mrs. Albert Watson, and Miss Marjorie Eede, both of Ballston Spa; a son, Arner G Eede, Lallston Spa; a sister, Mrs. John W. Weddell, New York, and a brother, ( arles H. Grose, sr.

# The Hortons

The Hortons were among the first to settle in Ballston Spa, their ancestry extending to Hebron, Connecticut, and the Revolutionary War. From Ezekial Horton II's arrival in the 1790s to James Horton's decades of public service, the family helped shape the civic and spiritual life of Saratoga County. Their legacy includes pioneers, clerks, soldiers, and dedicated community members, each generation building upon the reserved strength of the last.

Ezekial II (1768–1843) was a pioneer, settler, son, husband, and father. Ezekial's parents were Ezekial Horton and Lydia Shipman. He had five siblings: Philena, Russel, Shipman, Isabella, and Olive.

Ezekial married Annis Peters around 1787, and they settled in Connecticut. The Hortons settled in Ballston around the year 1795. Annis and Ezekial had one son, Elijah. Annis passed away in 1802, and she was interred in Briggs Cemetery in Ballston Spa. At the time of her death, she was merely in her late thirties.

Ezekial then married Clarissa Watson. (See Women of Worth for more information on Clarissa Watson Horton). Ezekial is buried in the Ballston Spa Village Cemetery, next to his wife, Clarissa, who passed away in 1839.

Elijah (1796–1870) married Anna Milliman in 1816. They lived in Galway in 1850 and in Broadalbin in 1855. John Milliman, Hiram, Wesley, Oscar, John Wesley, Melinda, Selena, Matilda, and Virginia were the children of Elijah and Anna. Elijah died in East Fishkill at 74. Anna later died in 1883.

JAMES W. HORTON.

James (1810-1885) married Abba Clark, his first wife, in 1836. He married his second wife, Julia Betts, in 1852. James, a druggist, left his work when he began working for Saratoga County as the clerk for 39 years. He got his education from the Ballston Academy. He served his church, The Methodist Episcopal Church, and was a member of the vestry for 40 years. In 1840, he was appointed postmaster of Ballston and held the office three years. During 1845, he became Saratoga County Clerk on the Whig Ticket, and through subsequent elections retained the job since, having been elected fourteen times to fill the same responsible role. He was a Whig in politics until the dissolution of that partisan.

James passed away at his home at 75. James and his family members are all buried in the Ballston Spa Village Cemetery.

James Clark (1837–1907) married Hannah "Fannie" Blish in 1867. James was in the Civil War during the raid on the Lawrence Massacre, which  was a defining moment in the border conflict. He established a drug company and then was employed by the United States Express and Wells-Fargo companies. James was a Kansas state representative and treasurer of the safety commission.

Captain Stephen Horton (1840–1887) was a captain with the Seventy-seventh New York Volunteers, receiving a wound at the Battle of Antietam.

Private William Horton (1842–1862) served in the Civil War, and was injured at the Second Bull Run, passed away from his injury in Washington, D.C. He was only 19 years old.

Captain Stephen S. Horton.

Clara Virginia (1849–1917) married George Beecher, a Saratoga County clerk. He was buried with Masonic honors. The couple shared three children: James, Willie, and Frances.

Jennie (1853–1904) never married, and the only mentions of her are in the obituaries of her family members, and an 1860 Census record, taken when she was only 6 years old. Jennie died at 51.

Annie (1858–1931) married James Aldrich. Her husband died young; he was only 51. Annie lived on to be 73 years old. Her name was in the 1860 Census but listed as Anna instead of Annie. She was 2 years old at the time of that record. James and Annie had one child, Julia, born in 1883. Julia married

John Guess, and they had a child, David.

# The Lows

Cornelius Pietersen "Louw" (1670-1748) married Margaret Van Borsum (1679-1761) in 1695.

Cornelius II (1700–1777) married Johanna Gouverneur (1705–1763) in 1729. *The Cornelius Low* house is a historical landmark and still stands in Piscataway, New Jersey. It was built in 1741. Cornelius was an affluent merchant and shipper based in Raritan Landing, New Jersey. Together, the couple had twelve children.

Infant Low (1730) lived less than a year, without a name, but a memory all the same.

Isaac (1731–1791) aided the crown, by becoming a Tory throughout the Revolutionary War and got banished by the legislature, and he moved to England where he passed away.

Sara (1732–1804) was the wife of Hugh Wallace. Their union began in 1760, her life enduring beyond his, remembered in family.

Margaretta (1734–1753) walked lightly through this world, leaving traces only in memory and kinship. She lived 19 short years, but those years impacted her family, and their legacy.

Cornelius III (1736–1769) married Catherine Hude Low. The couple had three children: James, Johanna, and Maria.

Samuel (1737–1756), for nineteen short years, was a brother remembered in silence, his life woven into kinship.

Nicholas (1739–1826) married Alice Haliburton Fleming (1758–1818). Alice was previously married to Sampson Fleming. She had three children, Fleming, Augustus, and Alexander.

**Nicholas Low**

In the reticent clash of early settlements, Nicholas stood as both competitor and visionary. Whatever others built, such as hotels, merchant shops, or other businesses, he matched but made much larger. He erected structures of generous scale and refined comfort, shaping Ballston into a destination of fashionable retreat. His Sans Souci Hotel, grand in ambition, rose near a newly discovered spring, *Low's Well,* was soon to become one of the village's most beloved waters. The first spring, fifty feet south of today's Iron Springs, gained the name *Public Well*, a communal start to Ballston's reputation as a healing place.

Low's reach extended beyond commerce. In 1804, he built a home later known as the McMaster House, which stood until a fire in 1855. He gifted land to his congregation, the Baptist Church and Society of Ballston Springs, anchoring their presence near the heart of the village. When the railroad arrived, the church moved to land once held by Stephen Smith, another echo of transition.

Low's generosity shaped civic life as well. He offered land for the county courthouse and clerk's office, securing Ballston Spa's role as the county seat. His name entered the map, Low Street a silent tribute to his influence. In the wake of the Revolutionary War, he emerged as a founding figure, serving in the New York State Assembly and Legislature, investing in factories, hotels, and the future of the village.

Nicholas Low did not simply build, he gave. His legacy lives on in the springs, the streets, and the spaces where community gathered, healed, and grew.

Ann married John Johnstone, a descendant of New York mayor John Johnstone. Cornelius served as a Federalist in the 26th New York State Legislature.

Henrietta married Charles King (1789–1867), son of US Senator Rufus King. They had three children: Annie, Cornelius, and Augustus.

William, John, Johanna, Gertrude [1] and Gertrude [2] all died under the age of 8 years.

# The Smiths

SAMUEL SMITH.

Samuel (1780-1838), a pioneer among the initial merchant tailors, lived in Balls-Town. He began business here about the time the village became incorporated. His family was one of the first settlers. Samuel married Lucinda Watrous, daughter of Edward Watrous, another pioneer settler in the town.

Samuel and his family belonged to St. Paul's church. Samuel belonged to the Episcopal liturgy in Ballston Spa. Samuel's friends and fellow Episcopalians, Joshua Aldridge and Salmon Tryon were selected as Wardens, and Epenetus White, Jr., Samuel Smith, William Noble, John Smith Wright Tryon, Archibald Kidd, William Bridges and Nathan Parker, were all vestrymen. The congregation was "The Rector, Wardens and Vestrymen of St. Paul's Church in the village of Ballston Spa," but it eventually disengaged. The distinct congregations sustained only a weak life, and in 1817 it was merged into a single society, to be in the growing village of Ballston Spa.

Samuel and other pioneers made up part of the Masonic Lodge. In 1816, Samuel announced in the local paper he has moved his tailor shop "two doors east of the Ballston Spa bookstore, between those celebrated mechanics, Langworthy and Williams."

Lucinda (1788–1866) parents were Edward Allen Watrous Esq and Susanna Pierson. She had two brothers, Andrew, and Edward Jr. Lucinda began her life three years after Reverend Eliphalet Ball's acquisition of the land that became Ballston. Her father numbered amongst the original settlers, and her marriage to Samuel, positioned her at the core of the village's financial and social progress.

Lucinda, one of Ballston Spa's initial community and cultural components, helped the village's social and religious activities during its development. Though records are sparse, her presence in a prominent merchant family suggests influence on community building and legacy preservation. Samuel's tailor shop was a hub of local interaction. As his wife, Lucinda managed household affairs, supported the business, and participated in the rhythms of village life, hosting, organizing, and maintaining social ties. She was not just a name, more than a spouse and parent in history's shadow. Lucinda lived in the pulse of Ballston Spa as it grew from frontier to village, her days woven into the rhythm of commerce, kinship, and gentle faith.

In a town formed by mineral springs and millwork, Lucinda's fortitude was gentler, unearthed in the quiet of Sunday mornings, the folding of linens for church gatherings, the whispered prayers for neighbors and kin. She sat in the pews.

Her burial in Ballston Spa Village Cemetery, in a marked plot near the fence, indicates enduring local respect. She lived through the rise of Ballston Spa's mineral springs industry, rail lines, and the transformation of the village into a county seat.

Charlotte (1810–1882) married Wheeler Booth (1806-1877), and the two were both devout Christians, and members of the Christ Church. They had five children, Margaret, Sarah, Samuel, Andrew, and Mary.

Margaret, lived in Ballston Spa throughout her life, belonged to Christ Church and a lady highly thought of by her friends. She was killed by being struck by the locomotive the was hauling the southbound Saratoga Limited, as she was crossing the track on an errand at the rear of her Front Street residence about midway between the Science and Walnut Street crossings.

Sarah was a lifelong resident of Ballston Spa Village. As a lifelong member of Christ Church, her actions showed Christian virtue. She married Horace Barnum Newton and together they had three children: Charlotte, Horace, and Samuel. Charlotte died from consumption.

Samuel lived 21 years. Samuel was named after his maternal grandfather.

Andrew was one of the first members of the Utopian Club when it began in 1885 and for many years functioned as its president. He had held the position of president of the Ballston Spa National Bank and the Ballston Spa Cemetery Association. Andrew worked as a telegraph operator for Western Union in Ballston Spa in the 1870's-1880's. (See Andrew Booth).

Mary married Mahlon Diehl (1848–1892) in 1886. She married John Royce Taverner (1848–1884). She and John had one child, Samuel Royce Taverner.

Andrew Sr. (1812–1886) married Emma Thompson (1836-1924), She was the daughter of George Thompson and Sarah Ann Wright in 1860. He was born in Ballston Spa, and when he turned 18, he went to New Orleans. He started a clerkship in the Banking House of Edward McMaster. Later, his brother, Samuel Smith, moved there as well, and they formed a banking house of Smith Brothers & Company. Upon the start of hostilities, rebels took gold held in their vault, leading to the bank's closure. They sued the General who sought out their gold and got it returned to them. Later, they moved back to Ballston Spa. Andrew purchased a mansion that was previously owned by Robert McMaster. Andrew and Emma had six children. Andrew, Samuel, George, Margaret, Roland, and Edward. Samuel married Mary Rathbon Baker Fithian (1865–1933). George Thompson married Mary J Potter Smith (1872–1960) in 1899. Margaret (1865) lived less than one year.

Edward (1873-1946) married Mildred Thompson (1874–1945) in 1898. They had three children, Mildred, Emmy, and Marjorie.

Alicia (1815–1853) is to be remembered as wife and companion to Samuel Wakeman. Their lives ended within a month of each other, now joined in rest at Ballston Spa Village Cemetery.

Mary Lucinda (1817–1902) married Dr. Leverett Moore (1805–1892). When she died, she held the title of oldest native resident of Ballston Spa. She belonged to the Christ Church. She had been a widow at her death, and her late husband, Dr. Moore, was a prominent physician for over fifty years.

Samuel Jr (1819–1884) returned with his brother, Andrew, to Ballston Spa, and then built a mansion on High Street and Ballston Avenue. He married Mary Adele Casey (1838-1912). The Smith brothers, including Andrew and Robert, were community cornerstones. Samuel and Mary had seven children: G. Montrose, Mary, Robert, Marguerite and Percy, with Sydney being the one who lived to adulthood.

When the war began, the Smith Brothers managed a thriving enterprise as bankers and cotton brokers. Following the city's capture, there were many thousands of dollars in gold within the vaults, which General Butler seized by order. The Smith's returned to Ballston Spa but at the close of the war, sued General Butler and, to recover their property. When they returned home, they managed the banking house until 1870. Sydney Smith, active in sports all his life, for many years maintained a stable of horses at High St. and Ballston Ave. He was a member of many clubs, including the Union and Colony and Saratoga Golf Club. During the organization of the Ballston Hounds, he was active in its hunts.

Sydney married Frances Tailer Carpenter in 1896. He married Florence Hathorn in 1926. He and Frances had two children, Sydney and Earl.

Ann (1821–1911) is remembered as a wife, a mother, and a daughter. She married Nathaniel Montross, raising Kate, her legacy carried forward in family bonds.

ROBERT P. SMITH.

Martha Susan (1823–1907) married Thomas Smithfield-Dugan. Their home in New Orleans was filled with family, raising Louise and Thomas, her long life remembered in love.

Robert (1827–1881), who had never married, yet remained close to his brothers. His life carried him from New Orleans back to Ballston Spa, where he lived until fifty-four.

# The Taylor Family

The Taylors' family ties were strong, famous for serving as judges and justices of the peace. Even across distance, and in a time that letters represented the only connection, they stayed in touch, probably through accurate writing and honest phrases. Sally Holmes counted as one of them, part of a lineage shaped by duty, loyalty, and enduring ties.

Judge John Taylor (1749-1829) was a Justice of the Peace, farmer, husband, father, and a man of strong faith. John was born in the county of Monmouth, New Jersey, and was the third lineal descendant of Edward Taylor of England, one of the emigrants for civil and religious liberty during the reign of James II.

*Judge John Taylor*

John married Chloe Cox in 1773. They moved from England to America and settled in Charlton in 1774. John became a farmer. John was a longtime county court judge from 1809 to 1818. John had two siblings, William and Joseph. John and his wife had seven children: Richard, William, Edward, John, Elizabeth, Sally, and Anna. The Taylor family has a very extensive family tree, and they were a prominent family, where they had a devout faith, and a thirst for knowledge, and justice, as well as a community. John was a member of the Presbyterian Church, Charlton Town Supervisor and a Justice of the Peace. John's parents were Joseph Taylor and Elizabeth Ashton Taylor. He had two siblings, William and Joseph Taylor Jr.

John's family always honored their ancestors and various generations, by continuing to carry on not only first names or middle names but adding the wife's maiden name as one of their children's first or middle name, or the maiden name of a previous generation.

Joseph (1775-1829) married Mary Henry, and they had two children. Mary and John. Joseph was a merchant and was appointed to a confidential position within the US Post Office in Washington DC, where he lived for the rest of his life.

Mary (1803-1872) never married but was a successful teacher. She was appointed to the Post Office Department position.

John (1815-1836) was a scholar. He graduated from Union College. He was admitted to the bar before he was 21, but he accidentally drowned when riding his horse across Cotoco Creek.

Richard (1777-1847) married Peninah Hawley (1781–1803). They had one son, Anson and daughter, Sally. He married his second wife, Mrs. Holmes, and their child was Obadiah. Richard's third wife was Sophie Wright (1780-1810). Their children were John and Chloe. Richard married a fourth wife, Phebe Clark, a widow (1779–1858) and they had Elisha and James.

Anson Sr. (1800–1864) though unable to hear, was an exceptional businessperson, building infrastructure projects and railways in NY. Anson married Miss Dennison, and had two children, Mary and Anson Hawley, Jr. Anson Jr was in business with his father, until his father's death. Since Anson Sr, was deaf, he was killed while standing on the railroad track at Joliet, 111., by a train of cars in 1864.

Sally (1802-1802) was named after her aunt Sally Taylor Holmes. Sally lived six months, leaving an empty cradle and a small legacy behind.

Obadiah (1803-1812) only lived 9 years, but his life and memory created a loss and yet, fond memories from his family.

John Wright (1808–1843) married three times; his first two wives dyed before having children. He was named after his uncle John. In 1840, he married Mary Bancroft, who had one son, Edward (1841-1861) enlisted in the first California Regiment in Philadelphia. He lost his left hand in the battle of Ball's Bluff in 1861; was discharged in 1862 for disability. In 1864, Edward married Maria Newcomb, and they moved to Milwaukee, Wisconsin, and in 1869 to Port Huron, Michigan. They have five children: Cornelia, Edith, John, Edward, and Paul.

Chloe (1810-1900) married James Callen in 1825. Together, they purchased the homestead once belonging to John Taylor, establishing their own family roots. Their children were Sarah [1] (lived 8 years), John, James, Richard, Sarah [2], Levi [1] (lived less than a year), Elizabeth, Levia (named for her late brother) lived less than a year, Levi [2], Edward, Mary, Georgiana.

Levi's [2] obituary stated that "The Eagle Valley Enterprise, CO. … a veteran of the Civil War. He and his wife moved to Leadville … in 1879 … a member of the Grand Army of the Republic, the only surviving member in Rifle, and a life member of the Masonic order.

Richard Jr. was the child of Richard's fourth wife. He was killed by a falling tree in a whirlwind. The only record that could be found about Richard Jr, was the Taylor Genealogy Document.

Elisha (1815-1874) entered the ministry and married Mary Perkins in 1840. They raised nine children together. Albert, Morgan, James, Charles, Mary, Electus, Grace, William, and Louise.

After Mary Jane's passing, Elisha later wed Adra Fessenden Bradbury. He founded the Strong Place Baptist Church, a mission in South Brooklyn devoted to community and faith. Elisha died of typhoid fever at his summer residence in Marlboro, New York.

James (1818-1892) owned a business as a dry goods merchant. He married Charlotte Davis in 1840. He opened the first saleratus (key ingredient in baking powder, also known as sodium bicarbonate) factory in Delphi. They moved to Brooklyn and became among the most successful businessmen, "characterized by great energy and persistence and boundless hospitality." James and Charlotte had two children, Laura and Charlotte. Laura's husband, Charles Pope, went into business with James. Charlotte married George Doheny, Esq., but she passed away just two years after they married.

William (1779-1836) married Lucy Embry Harger in 1806. William, a farmer, held the positions of justice of the peace, town supervisor for Charlton, and an elder in the Presbyterian Church. William and Lucy had thirteen children; Lillie, James, William, Eber, John, Ann, Sarah, Elisha, David, Richard, Josiah, Lydia "L.J." and Joseph.

Edward (1781-1867) married Eunice Curtis, and together they raised a large family of nine children. John, Ann Maria, Luzerne, Phebe, Elisha, William, Jane, Clara, and Susan. (Also, see the Curtiss family.)

Honorable John W. (1784-1854) married Jane Hodge, and together they had six children: Sarah Jane, James, Malvina, John II, Oscar, and Edgar. Raised in a

household where law and public service were guiding principles, his father, John followed in those footsteps. He attended Union College and pursued the study of law, eventually establishing his practice in Ballston Spa, New York.

According to the document of the descendants of the Taylors, Jane Hodge was "a beautiful woman, attractive, courageous, practical, efficient, with great delicacy and tact."

Beyond the courtroom, John was deeply committed to education and civic life. He helped found the Ballston Center Academy and served as a local justice, reflecting his dedication to community building. His integrity and sense of duty led him into politics, where he represented his district in Congress during a time of shifting ideologies and national change. After years of public service, he returned to the practice of law and later settled in Ohio, embracing a quieter life grounded in the values of family, perseverance, and principles.

Sarah (1808-1857) Sarah, married William Beattie (1802–1861). They had eight children: Mary Jane, Malvina, Elizabeth, Sarah Louise, Julia, Cornelia, William, and Henry.

James (1809-1835) served in the Indian Wars with the 5th Regiment Infantry. His life ended tragically when he drowned in the Cossitol River in Arkansas, approximately seventy miles from Fort Towson.

Elizabeth (1812-1878) married Thomas Robertson in 1843. Thomas became a prominent banker in Rockford, and then a large landholder. They had six children, and only two survived to adulthood, William and Mary.

Malvina (1815-1899) graduated from the Female Seminary in Ballston Spa. She married Dr. Edward Taylor in 1839. After spending several years in Mississippi. They settled in Cleveland, Ohio, where Edward died in 1868. After Edward's death, she spent time with her brothers, and they moved back to Ballston Spa and was active in her church.

Lieutenant Colonel John William Taylor II (1817-1902) served with distinction as a lieutenant colonel in the Volunteers Quartermaster's Department during the Civil War. He got a position on the staff of Generals John Pope and William Rosecrans and later became Chief Quartermaster of the Army of the Cumberland under Rosecrans. He was made a captain and assistant quartermaster in 1861; he rose in rank in 1862 but gave up his position the next year because of poor health. John married Anna Sexton in 1848, and she died in 1849 in childbirth, leaving one child, Anna Louisa (1849). He married Clara Cushing in 1853, who died in 1868. He married Sarah Gushing in 1871. They had one child, Edith.

Charles (1820-1847) graduated from Union College in 1839. He studied law at Ballston Spa Law School. After he passed the bar, he practiced law in Alabama and lived in Snow Hill until his death.

Oscar (1822–1909) was a prominent banker and attorney in Freeport, Illinois. In 1852, he established Freeport's first bank, marking a significant milestone in the town's development. His home, known as the *Oscar Taylor House*, became a vibrant social and cultural hub, welcoming many distinguished guests.

During the American Civil War, the house served a deeper purpose, it became a station on the Underground Railroad. Escaped slaves were protected in the basement, concealed by a hidden door disguised with shelving. That door still stands as a quiet testament to courage and compassion. The residence remained in the Taylor family until 1944, then it was given as a gift to create the Stephenson County Historical Society and changed into a historic house museum. Oscar married Malvina Snow, and together they had six children. Mary Malvina, Elizabeth who was twins with Mary Malvina, Winifred Louise, Oscar Livingstone, Malvina Snow, and Charissa.

Elisha (1786-1861) started providing for himself when he was thirteen, demonstrating his tenacity and fortitude. He pursued higher education at Union College and later established a mercantile business in Schenectady. Elisha first married Ann Dunlop and moved to Ohio, where Ann passed away in 1824. Two years later, he married Elizabeth Ely, and the couple moved to Cherry Valley before returning to Schenectady.

He embraced the emerging temperance movement, adopting total abstinence from alcohol and advocating for its principles. A devoted member of the Presbyterian Church, he gave generously, nearly a quarter of his annual net profits, to support its mission. His faith and leadership extended into public service; he served as an officer in the War of 1812.

Elisha joined the forty-three founders of the Jefferson Avenue Presbyterian Church, aiding in building its beautiful sanctuary. He shortly became one of its elders and played a key part in bringing in the idea of "rotary eldership," a method later supported by the General Assembly. He served as an elder for over twenty years, dedicating himself to the spiritual and ministerial life of the church. Elisha and Elizabeth had two children, Alfred and Louisa.

Elizabeth "Betsey" (1788-1886) married Nathan Seeley, a farmer, in 1811. "She had the best educational advantages the country afforded [...]. Her husband was drafted as a soldier in the War of 1812. They resided in Carlisle, and Charlestown, NY. He became a deacon in the Baptist Church. Their house was a haven of rest to many a weary minister of the Gospel, and a very hospitable home. Her husband died May 5, 1862, at Syracuse," and she lived with her eldest son, Rev. John T Seeley, a prominent Baptist clergyman in western NY, until her death. Together, they had five children: John, Jesse, Anna Eliza, David, and Chloe.

John (1814-1903) followed a path of faith and became a reverend, continuing the family's legacy of service and spiritual leadership. John was the pastor of Pittsford Baptist Church, New York. He graduated from Madison University in 1839, and then from Baptist Theological Seminary in 1841. John was ordained as a minister of the Gospel. He married Harriet in 1841. He stopped his pastoral life and never went back. However, during his time as a pastor, he baptized 1100 people and performed marriage ceremonies for about 1,000 people. Though he left being a pastor, he was an active Christian.

Jesse (1815-1896) followed a path of religion and became a reverend, continuing the family's legacy of service and spiritual leadership. Jesse moved to Iowa. He was licensed to be a preacher, and then spent nine years as a teacher, preacher and student. In his lifetime, he organized 15 churches and was a pastor in 8 of them. He had to stop being a reverend when he lost his voice. He married Sarah in 1847. Sarah died in 1848. He married Agnes Scott. She died in 1857. His third wife was Mrs. Gulaelma Pier in 1860. Jesse's children were Adelaide, Oscar, John, Emma, Hattie, Jessie, Jessie, Anna, who married

Rev. T. G. Lamb, and Harriet.

Their son, David (1821-1903) married Maria Loucks. He owned a business in Albany. They had four sons: John Nathan, Harvey, Jane, and William.

Their daughter Chloe married Matthew Freeman, who was an editor. They had five children, including Elizabeth, married to Alfred Widener, who was a farmer. John was an editorial reporter, and he married his colleague. Charles moved to Ohio. Anna married George Morris. They had three children when Mr. Morris died, and Anna had to get a job as a teacher to support her family. Hattie married Joseph Kelly.

Sally (1792-1840) married Daniel Holmes, a farmer, in 1811. They moved to Lake Ontario and had to suffer privations, hardships, and poverty of frontier life, and live the life of a Christian. She was the mother of 13 children, with ten surviving. As a thoroughly dedicated Christian, her faith sustained her even through the toughest times. Sally and Daniel's children were Sarah, Richard, William (who lived six years), James (who only lived two years), Ezra, Elisha, George, Mary, James, Daniel Jr., Lucy(who lived 14 years), Lydia.

Sally's children who survived to adulthood married and had children, giving Sally the gift of being a grandmother.

Anna (1794-1940) married Ezra Sprague, a merchant, in 1815. Though Ezra faced long-standing health issues and financial hardship, together they raised five children: David, William, Mary, Anna, and Sarah. Their story reflects hushed perseverance through adversity, and the enduring strength of family ties.

Taylor Family Motto: *Consequitor quodctuique petit*, "He accomplishes what he undertakes."

RESIDENCE OF JOHN W. TAYLOR.
Now the Home of John Brown.

# The Thompsons

The Thompsons, a family of pioneers, judges, and civic stewards, were grounded in Stillwater and Milton, but part of Saratoga County's larger structure. From Captain John Thompson's Revolutionary service to Judge James Thompson's decades on the bench, their legacy comprised leadership and public trust. Their heirs, including Rhoda Thompson, carried forward that tradition with reserved strength, supporting education, charity, and community life. Rose Hill, the family homestead, stood as both symbol and sanctuary, a place where intellect, care, and continuity endured across generations.

Captain John Thompson (1745-1823) was born in Litchfield, within the Connecticut Colony, John

moved with his family to Stillwater at fourteen. There, he became a farmer and one of the early pioneers of Saratoga County. He married Fanney, and together they raised three children: Martha, William, and

John W. Thompson

James.

Service and leadership characterized John's life. He served as a captain and company commander in the 13th Regiment of the Albany County Militia during the American Revolution, including active duty in both battles of Saratoga. His civic contributions continued long after the war, appointed Justice of the Peace in 1788, elected to the New York State Assembly in 1788 and 1789, and commissioned as First Judge of Saratoga County in 1791.

In 1798, John was elected to Congress as a Democratic-Republican, serving one term from 1799 to 1801.

John retired to Stillwater, where he lived out his remaining years. He passed away at 78, leaving behind a legacy of patriotism, public service, and perseverance.

Martha (1771–1816) lived a life grounded in family and reserved strength. She became the second wife of Aaron Gregory, and later settled in Milton Center, where she passed away at approximately 44 years of age. Her will designated her brothers as executors, reflecting the Thompson family's enduring connection.

William (1785-1871) lived an abiding life. Mary Hawkins became his wife, and they raised Edwin and Nancy. William died in 1871 at the age of 86, and was buried in Ovid Union Cemetery, ending a life of family and stability.

James (1775–1845) served as First Justice of Saratoga County from 1818 to 1833, shaping the region's legal establishment with wisdom and integrity. In 1806, he purchased a farm in Milton, just northwest of Ballston Spa, which became known as the Judge Thompson place, later Rose Hill Farm. There, he built the homestead that would remain central to the family's story.

James first married Rhoda Thompson, and together they had three children: George, John Whalen, and Mary. After Rhoda's passing at 42, James married Mary Stansbury, with whom he had three more children: Rhoda, James, and Edward.

James passed and was interred in the Ballston Spa Village Cemetery. His widow, Mary, later moved in with their daughter Rhoda at Rose Hill. Though Mary became blind in her later years, her daughter's devoted care brought light and comfort to her closing chapter. Mary lived to the age of 92, passing in 1889, a silent testament to the strength and tenderness that defined the Thompson home.

Rhoda Thompson

Rhoda (1834–1923) inherited Rose Hill from her father, a home built with care and purpose. Despite never marrying, Rhoda continued her family's tradition of intelligence and community involvement, managing her wealth with skill and elegance. She stayed involved in her community, backing local charities and privately paying for the West Milton District School's maintenance and upgrades.

Rhoda died, and her relatives then spread out from New York State. Her cousin, Miss Edith Smith of Virginia, and her dear friend, Miss Lucy Bateman, provided loving care in her final days. In 1923, Rhoda passed away and was buried in the Ballston Spa Village Cemetery. The final farewell took place in serene decorum, a reflection of the existence she experienced, true, giving, and deeply connected.

Captain Edward Davis Thompson (1837–1906) moved to Lawrence, Kansas in 1857 and engaged in the private banking business. He, too, had an interest in the Lawrence Bridge Co. until the state rescinded its charter and made it a free bridge. He enlisted in the Second Kansas Volunteers [infantry] at the opening of the Civil War. His role as adjutant of the regiment caused him to be known as "Captain." He married Inez Hulin. Together, the couple had two children, Agnes and Bert.

James (1835–1885) joined the Grand Army of the Republic in 1862, where he served as an officer in the 155th Regiment. He served in Virginia during the Civil War.

John Whalen (1808-1892) succeeded in the judicial honors of the family, having been Surrogate of the county from 1834 to 1847. He was born at the family homestead in Milton. In 1835, he wedded Augusta Isabella Lee, a daughter of Joel Lee. Together, they had four children: George, Samuel, Alice, and Frank. He became a lawyer and got a partner. After James' resignation in 1856, he became president, having been a Ballston Spa Bank incorporator and a first board member. He focused on financial matters, and stayed president of the Ballston Spa National Bank until passing away. John W. was 84 when he died. He rests at the Ballston Spa Village Cemetery.

George Lee (1835–1895) married Caroline Agry Blish in 1876. They lived in Ballston Spa until his death. She served as the caretaker for her husband since, at the end of his life, he could not make decisions. Caroline Thompson came to life in Gardiner, Maine. She held an important position in the social circle of Saratoga Springs and Ballston Spa, sang for many years in the choir at Christ church. They had three children, Alice, Samuel, and Frank.

George Jr. (1803-1871) succeeded his father as president of the bank. He served two terms as Supervisor of Milton. He was the one child who took a spouse. George, the oldest sibling, a graduate of Union College, from the year 1822, served as County Treasurer four times; He married Sarah Ann

Wright Thompson. Together they had five children. Emma. John W, Eliza, Sarah, Fannie and Charles. George died at his home on Milton Avenue.

# The Watsons

Captain Titus Watson (1743–1820) Titus was a soldier and a farmer. He married Mercy Merrill in 1772. Her brother was James Merrill.

Watson wrote a letter to General George Washington[5]:

**"From Captain Titus Watson**
Camp P. Highlands [NY]
26th of June 1779.
May it please your Excellency,

*I am sorry to trouble your Excellency again upon the subject of my rank,1 neither would I do it were I not sensible that I have been materially injured and that ungenerous methods have been taken by a Gentleman of distinguished rank in the Connecticut Line to prevent justice taking place. I therefore think in justice to myself I am in duty bound to state the circumstances of the case, and desire that your Excellency will see my grievances amply redressed.*

*When the relative rank of Captains in the Connecticut Line was determined it was my misfortune to be absent, by which means Clift gained precedence. Major Throop who was in the same predicament and whose claims are similar with mine, considering himself injured applied for a rehearing, obtained it, and the rank of Clift: I therefore concluded that I should stand senior to him in the Arrangement then sent to the Board of War, and was not undeceived 'till I saw in Genl Orders Clift ordered to the duty of Major. I then waited on Genl Putnam and desired a rehearing which he refused to grant. being still dissatisfied, I obtained leave, went to the Board of War, stated my case, and was directed to return and make application to the Commandant of the Connecticut Line, who, upon exhibiting my directions from the Board thought proper to order a Court which was in these terms, Lt Colos. Johnson, Grosvenor and Major Torey, are to set as a Court to enquire into the disputed rank between Major Clift, and Capt'n Watson: the Court apprehended it inconsistent for them to determine upon this order and sent to the Genl, whether the Court was to consider our antecedent claims prior to Clifts promotion (which was*

---

[5] This letter was edited for spelling only.

*undoubtedly the intention of the Board of War), or whether they were strictly to adhere to the letter of the Order? the Genl did not think proper to make any alterations, and my claims were not considered.*

*I found that there was a combination formed against me, that Genl Parsons was bent upon baffling every effort of mine to obtain justice: for when he heard that I was gone to the Board of War he immediately dispatched a Letter to them with a design (as he himself publicly declared), to foil me. but it arrived too late. When the aforementioned Court sat, he wrote a Letter to them, intimating that it was much better for me to leave the Army than to make any disturbance. I can assure you of your Excellency that I never had the least intention of creating any disturbance: my motive was to obtain justice to myself, which every Officer has a right to do when injured in so delicate a point. After this no other resource appeared from whence there was the least prospect of gaining redress, but from your Excellency, I therefore wrote to your Excellency, requesting a rehearing, who was pleased to direct a Court to be ordered. before which my claim were stated and the determination was in my favour (as will appear by the enclosed certificate)2 and sent to Genl Putnam to forward to your Excellency, but I cannot learn that it ever was done, for I waited on the Genl to know whither he had sent the result of the Court forward, his answer was short and highly dissatisfactory: For several reasons I am led to believe that neither your Excellency nor the Board of War have ever received the doings of the last Court, also that they were not sent.*

*I have been in the Army from the beginning of the contest and have served my Country to the best of my abilities. I still wish to continue, could I do it with reputation; and why I have not as good a claim to justice as Major Throop and many others I am at a loss. Our pretensions are equal, he is right. I am Opposed by a Gentleman of extensive abilities, and of connections, whose line of conduct in an affair of this nature ought to be and to appear totally disinterested.*

*My connections are not numerous, unsupported by friends, having spent my small patrimony in the service of my Country, injured in a matter of a verry delicate nature; and now obliged to retire from a mode of life which corresponds with my inclinations. is too injurious. I therefore once more solicit your Excellency that my case may be taken into consideration, that justice take place, and I be able to continue to serve my Country with reputation to myself and Friends.4 I am with greatest respect Your*

*Excellency, your obedient humble Servant. Titus Watson, Capt."* [6]

He joined the Revolutionary War in April 1775, defending the Lexington Alarm as a sergeant from Bethlehem, Connecticut. Titus Watson's military experience, from the Boston march to the Quebec campaigns, followed the changing front lines of the young nation's fight for independence.

Serving as a lieutenant, he saw action at St. Johns, Montreal, and Chambly. His promotion to captain happened in February 1776. He fought at Brandywine, Germantown, and Monmouth during his six years of service. Standing at Valley Forge, he joined the 7th Connecticut, taking his oath.

Captain Watson endured the hardships of war, harsh winters, disease, and the brutal toll of battle. He witnessed the devastation of smallpox in the Northern Department and the sweltering heat of Monmouth, where exhaustion claimed nearly as many lives as musket fire. Yet among his many acts of courage, one stands apart.

While on reconnaissance near New Rochelle in 1779, Watson and his men ran into Simcoe's Rangers. Watson slew a light horseman in a close fight at night and guided his troops through swamps to Byram Bridge, which they took apart just in time.

With Tories in full hunt, Watson reached Horseneck and warned General Putnam of the approaching enemy. Putnam's narrow escape down the rocky bluff known as *Put's Hill* became legend, but it was Watson's warning that made it possible.

Titus Watson moved to Balls-Town, circa 1772, prior to the war. His name was listed as one of the first Freemasons in the area, appearing on the original roll of Franklin Lodge. James Watson, his younger brother, later served as a US Senator from New York and was appointed Naval Officer of the Port of New York by President John Adams.

After the war, Captain Watson returned to farming. In 1818, he was granted a pension for his service. His widow, Mercy, applied for and received support in 1836, at 87, while living in Watervliet, Albany County. She died two years later, on May 14, 1838.

Captain Watson's legacy lives patiently in the soil of Ballston and in the memory of a nation he

---

[6] https://founders.archives.gov/documents/Washington/03-21-02-0222

helped defend, resolute, brave, and true. Captain Watson's daughter Clarissa married Ezekial Horton.

# The Westcots & Lees

Marriage united the Wescot and Lee families, and they stayed connected through common values, work, service, and community links. The civic and commercial heart of the village was shaped by the lives of Joseph Westcot, Joel Lee and others, including Westcot's early presence in Ballston Spa and Lee's work as a merchant tailor, postmaster, and Justice of the Peace.

Their legacy was continued by their descendants through banking, law, military service, education, and care. Augusta Lee's marriage to John Whalen Thompson tied the family to a distinguished Saratoga County legal and financial heritage. The Ballston Spa National Bank thrived for many decades under the leadership of John Joseph Lee, George Lee Thompson Sr., and others. Rhoby Barnum and her daughters expanded the family's reach, establishing themselves in new locations and careers, from Cleveland to California.

  Joseph Esq. (1754–1795) moved from Stephentown to Ballston Spa in 1795, accompanied by Reuben Hewitt. That same year, he married Reuben's daughter, Priscilla, and together they became part of the village's early fabric. Joseph and Reuben purchased the hotel formerly owned by Benajah Douglas, marking their place in Ballston's growing civic and social life. Joseph's story reflects the soft beginnings of a family rooted in partnership, hospitality, and community ties.

Priscilla (1763–1839) first married Joseph Westcot, with whom she had six children. After Joseph's passing, she married Joshua Aldridge in 1796, and together they had two more children. Through both marriages, Priscilla helped shape two family legacies rooted in hospitality, resilience, and community ties. She lived a life of devotion and adaptability, bridging generations with grace. Priscilla passed in 1839 and is buried in Briggs Cemetery.

Patience (1784–1866) married Joel Lee, a merchant tailor and goods store owner in Ballston Spa.

Together they raised eight children and built a life grounded in service and community. Joel served as postmaster and Justice of the Peace for the town of Milton, reflecting the family's commitment to civic duty.

Their daughter Emeline married David White in 1822, continuing the family's local ties. Their son Edward, once a leading businessman in Ballston, operated a store at the corner of Front and Bath Streets, later the site of the First National Bank. Though Edward lived with paralysis for nearly a decade, he remained a figure of strength and perseverance. He married Anna Williams in 1831.

Patience passed and left behind a legacy of family, faith, and soft fortitude.

Augusta (1811–1871) married John Thompson, whose lineage and leadership shaped Saratoga County's civic and financial life. John, the grandson of Judge John Thompson, selected in 1791 as the county's first judge of the Court of Common Pleas, and He was the beloved son of Judge James Thompson, who kept the same office from 1818 to 1836.

Augusta and John's sons were George, Alice, Samuel, and Frank. Augusta's death in 1871 resulted in a legacy of family strength and civic continuity.

George Sr. followed in his father's footsteps, serving as president of the Ballston Spa National Bank. Before assuming the presidency, he worked for many years as teller and cashier, gaining the trust and respect of the community. He inherited a substantial estate from his father and continued the family's tradition of financial leadership and public service.

GEORGE L. THOMPSON.

Lucy (1814–1883) married George Scott, and together they raised two children: Caroline and James. Lucy's life bridged generations of civic-minded, community-rooted families, and her legacy continued through her children and grandchildren.

Her daughter Caroline married Charles McCreedy in 1871. They had two sons: Gordon and Charles Jr. Her son James married Anna Boone in 1896, and they had one child, Gordon. Through these branches,

Lucy's lineage extended into new chapters, carrying forward the values of family, faith, and soft perseverance.

Lucy passed in 1883, remembered as a matriarch whose life wove together the enduring threads of the Wescot and Lee families.

John Joseph (1817–1887) began his working life as a goldsmith, a trade that reflected in precision and artistry. In 1839, he got the teller position at the Ballston Spa National Bank, and in 1855, he took on its cashier role. His steady existence and financial intelligence helped guide the bank through decades of growth.

John had strong engagement in civic and fraternal life, acting as a charter member of Franklin Lodge F. & A.M., within which he held a notable position in Masonic circles. He married Mary Jane in 1842, though she passed just a year later. He later married Almena Burton (1818–1888), and together they had one daughter, Isabella. When John passed he was remembered for his dedication to craft, community, and family.

Mary (1819–1896) married Nathaniel Clark, and together they had five children: Horace, Joel Lee, Elizabeth, Mary, and Isabella. Of their children, only two survived into adulthood, a testament to the fragility and strength that marked Mary's life. In both happiness and sadness, she was a constant, defined by family and faith. Mary was remembered for her grace, and her children kept her legacy alive.

Frances (1823–1913) married Callender Beecher in 1843. They had three children: George, John, and Ella. Callender, a promising young lawyer, journeyed to California during the Gold Rush of 1849 but died shortly after arriving. Frances later married John McLean, a paper manufacturer, and outlived both of her husbands.

Frances was considered one of Ballston Spa's most respected citizens upon her death. Through periods of change and hardship, her life showed resilience and family bonds.

George (1825–1879) chose a quieter path. He resided a great distance from the village, a location known by his title, and led a life not fully documented, yet not without experience. He found his final rest in his homeland's soil, not seeking any acclaim. His softly spoken story is a continuing part of the Lee family's legacy.

Rhoby Harris (1785–1869) married Eli Barnum, and together they had four daughters: Frances, Eunice, Rhoby, and Helen. Through these daughters, Rhoby's legacy extended into families marked by service, resilience, and civic engagement.

Her daughter Frances married Robert Pierson McMaster in 1831, and they had two children: Elizabeth and Rhobie. Eunice married James Savage in 1840 at the Episcopal Christ Church in Ballston Spa. James was a trader, and they had four children: James, Egbert, Frances, and Jenny. At the outbreak of the Civil War, both sons joined the Union Army. Egbert continued as a career officer, while James later took a position in Louisiana. After Rhoby's passing in 1869 at 83, the Savage family relocated to Cleveland, where James partnered in an insurance firm with William Albert Ludlum, who had married their daughter Fanny.

Rhoby's daughter Rhoby married James Madison Marvin (1809–1901), and they had four children: Mary, Frances, William, and Rhoby. Her youngest daughter, Helen, married William Dorlon.

Rhoby's life bridged generations of civic-minded families, and her legacy lived on through daughters and grandchildren who carried forward her strength, grace, and silent influence.

Eunice (1787–1872) married Harvey Loomis (1782–1857). They had three children. Joseph, Joshua, and Rhobie.

Joshua married Hester Noxon Hovey in 1843, and had one child, Davis.

Rhobie was named after her maternal aunt. She married John Peck. They had six children, Loomis, Duncan, James, Ida, Rhobie, Sargent, and Eunice.

Captain Reuben Westcot (1791-1862) got his name from his father's brother and his mother's father.

He volunteered at the start of the War of 1812 and was later promoted to captain. Following the war's end, he came back to Ballston Spa, and in 1815, he established a general store. The store he built in 1818, next to the First National Bank, was later used by his grandson, H. C. Westcot. In 1841, Mr. Westcot discontinued selling his dry goods and groceries and became a druggist. He married Phebe Howard (1798–1834) and the couple had four children. Sarah, Mary, John, and Joseph. For many years he was a member of Christ church, and one of its vestrymen. People recognized him as an enterprising businessman, and he received high regard as a citizen. He held a trusteeship for the village of Ballston Spa, for seven years, served as coroner of the county, and held the office of village president in 1851 and 1855.

REUBEN WESTCOT.

He died in 1862. His wife, Phebe Hart Howard, predeceased him and passed away in 1834.

Sarah (1818–1906) married Lorenzo Kelly (1817–1892) in 1841. They had four children, who lit up the homestead. Howard, James, Mary, and John. Sarah and Lorenzo lived most of their lives in Niagara Falls, NY.

Mary (1820–1872) never married. She lived in Ballston Spa her entire life. She was close to her family, who still lived in the area. She passed away at the age of 52.

John (1823–1895) spent his entire life in his native village, earning, and deserving, the confidence and esteem of all who knew him. He took over his father's business and ran it successfully until he passed away. As a dedicated member of Christ Church, he was on the vestry and junior warden for his final decade. He was dedicated to the community, serving in various roles: trustee, president, and on the Board of Education.

Joseph (1827–1902) was named after his grandfather. From 1847 to 1852, he worked as a copyist in the county clerk's office, starting his public service. In 1871, after working in New Orleans for several years, he returned to Ballston Spa and again worked in the county clerk's office, assisting in re-indexing official records. Joseph served with distinction as deputy county clerk for two decades. For two terms, he acted as trustee for the village. He showed remarkable efficiency and dedication while performing as deputy clerk. He died at the age of 75.

Frances Barnum (1830–1897) named for her Aunt Frances Barnum. She married Nathan Jewett Johnson in 1851, and together they raised three children: Mary, Edward, and Frank.

Stephen (1796–1796) was named in honor of his uncle Stephen. He died before he turned one, a milestone that his parents missed, along with his cooing and light giggles.

Eliza (1797–1798) died before she turned 1-year-old, like her older brother, Stephen. Their parents suffered another loss of an infant who had a promising future.

Norman (1802–1823) died at 21, just quite an adult, but his loss left a lingering hole in his parents, his family's heart.

# The Wests

George West guided the West family, who brought industry, faith, and philanthropy to Ballston Spa. George and Louisa moved from England and established a community-focused life through George's paper mill and their Methodist church involvement. The family's kindness, seen in donations for a new organ, city monuments, and church needs, went beyond worship. They are remembered for their business and long-term civic duty.

George (1823–1901) was a patriarch, father, husband, industrialist, and politician. George was born in Bradninch, England. George attended the common schools; immigrated to America in 1849 and settled at Ballston Spa. George served as a politician and an industrialist. He and his wife settled in Ballston Spa in 1861. He constructed nine different water-powered mills located on the Kayaderosseras Creek. In 1879, he was already making cotton, paper, and paper bags. He got the

**George West.**

The Republican candidate for the Assembly in the lower district of Saratoga, as heretofore stated, is Hon. George West, the excellent member of last winter. Mr. West is a faithful and unswerving Republican, a sagacious and successful business man, and served his constituents last session with great acceptability. So popular is he and so hopeless is any effort to beat him, that the opposition have made no nomination against him. They are wise in not wasting their labor.—*Alb. Eve. Journal.*

name "The Paper Bag King" because he initiated paper bag creation, instead of cotton material. He made the bags from manila paper that originated from manila hemp, selling the bags for a more affordable price than the cotton bag competition. He achieved remarkable success, and he either purchased or bought new mills. He held a position in the State assembly 1872-1876.

George and his wife, Louisa Rose, had six children, with only three surviving to adulthood. Infant

West, Infant West, George Jr., Charles, Walter, and Florence.

He gained recognition as a philanthropist, giving funds to construct a museum in Round Lake, NY, a Methodist church in Ballston Spa, and providing generous support towards the two soldiers' monuments in Saratoga County, in Ballston Spa and Schuylerville. He was a man who gave help in all ways possible, and ready to share his time and money for the betterment of the village or a cause he believed in.

In 1901, West died at his mansion in Ballston Spa, and less than a year later, Louisa died as well. They are buried in the Ballston Spa Village Cemetery.

George Jr. (1845-1906) married Emily Hathorn (1847-1913), and they had three children. George Jr. He engaged in commerce alongside his father and his spouse's sibling, Mr. Mabee. Worked in the family's paper mill business, which included multiple mills along Kayaderosseras Creek and a bag factory in Rock City Falls. While not as publicly prominent as his father, George Jr. held managerial or operational responsibilities within the mill complex, especially during its peak years.

Frederick (1874-?) married Clara. Clara filed for divorce in 1909. Frederick made a name for himself, but not in an effective way. He had money problems, and he drank regularly. He and his brother, Walter, didn't inherit any money from their father's estate because of their inability to handle their finances. Frederick "Fred" was in the military in 1898 during the Spanish-American War.

Charles (1850-1851) died at 10 months. His life was cut short, leaving behind empty arms of his parents, but his memory lived on in their hearts.

Walter (1875-1924) led a life marked by both turbulence and transformation. Struggles with alcohol in his early years ultimately led to his exclusion from his father's inheritance. At 21, he married Anne McPherson, and together they had two daughters, Emily and Dorothy. The marriage ended in divorce.

Later, Walter became involved with Grace Zweifel Usher, a married woman with a child. The relationship drew public attention when Grace's husband sued Walter for "alienation of affection," seeking $75,000, a case that made headlines. Despite the scandal, Walter and Grace eventually married.

After Grace's passing, Walter remarried once more, this time to Mary Hackett Lee. In his later years, he settled into a quieter life, leaving behind a legacy shaped by both controversy and change.

Florence (1856-1934) married Douglass Williams Mabee (1848–1929), a businessman who worked alongside her father and brother, George Jr.

Florence Louise West Mabee

Florence and Douglass raised seven children, each carrying forward the family's legacy in their own way. Their son, George, married Blanche Aiken Wiley in 1904, while Douglass wed Edna Marvin in 1907 and became father to Mirabel, Edna, and Douglas. Alfred remained a bachelor, living a reserved life that spanned eighty years. Florence married Ranulf Compton in 1907, and Louise married William Pennebaker Boone, with whom she had two children, Douglass and Florence. David served in World War I from 1917 to 1918 before marrying Elizabeth O'Connor McCarthy in 1934. Margaret married Charles Furness in 1920, continuing the family's story into a new generation.

Florence's life was deeply rooted in family and soft resilience. Through her children and grandchildren, the West and Mabee names remained woven into the fabric of community.

# The Wiswalls

Henry (1810–1882) was born to Samuel Wiswall and Nancy Boyer. Sadly, Henry's parents passed away the same year he was born. Henry's siblings included James, Anna, and Elizabeth. After their

marriage, Henry and Eunice Rymph parented eight children. In 1810, Henry appeared in the Mohawk Valley, and he developed as Ballston Spa transformed. He lived through canals expanding, railroads coming, and the city uniting. Henry and Eunice, proponents of Ballston Spa's 19th-century public and moral life, are recalled not just for their family but for their continued influence on village ethics.

He rests at Ballston Spa Village Cemetery, with his wife Eunice, signifying a long and respected time in the community. His gravestone marks not just a life lived, but a legacy quietly woven into the town's foundations.

Henry's name appears in local burial records and family histories, showing stable landholding and generational continuity.

Eunice (1824-1907) was part of the church community, seasonal rhythms, and social gatherings that shaped village life. As wife and mother, her work was a quiet dedication to hosting, care, and preserving family history. Despite a lack of official records, her burial spot by Henry shows a connection of respect and belonging.

Elizabeth (1840–1919) married Royal Stearns Sutfin. Together they had three children, Harry, Lillian, and Arthur. Henry married Annie Sutfin Mills (1870–1918).

Lillian originated from Troy. She graduated from the Hudson River Academy, NY. She married William Clirehugh (1853–1910), and they had one child, Robert.

Arthur Sutfin (1872-1946) married Louisa Hyde Sutfin (1875–1943). They had three children, Lillian, William, and Robert.

Eugene (1841–1912) moved to Saratoga county in 1864 and started farming. He later went into the lumber business, and teamed up with Mr. CB Thomas and Charles Spaulding for coal. His knowledge of farming and lumbering, and experience, led to him becoming the superintendent of the Saratoga County Agricultural society for a long time. A section of his farm in Saratoga Springs was called "The Geysers". He then relocated to South Broadway but continued to oversee his farm's operations. He owned a sawmill on Lake Avenue when he died of heart failure. He married Clara E VanEps (1848–1928).

Alice (1849–1929) married David Wood (1846-1911), and had one child, Wesley. Alice and David showed a high level of interest in Ballston Spa's business. The family lived on High Street until he died in 1911. She was important at Milton Grange, from its 1890 founding. She passed away while serving as an officer for Pomona Grange at Saratoga Springs.

Emma (1852–1919) married George Aldrich (1850-1881) and later, John Bently (1830-1924). She had one child with George. She had been born in Fort Miller and lived in North Milton with her family. Her home was across the street from Stone Church. She kept remarkably busy in the Methodist church, and she, such as her sister, Alice, a visible presence in activities of Milton Grange, since it's organization in 1890.

Clarence was a native of Ballston Spa; Mr. Aldrich served as district manager for the National Biscuit Co. in Florida. He held membership and had served as a trustee of First Methodist Church. He married Rose McVeigh in 1906. He married Adelaide Aldrich in 1921. They had one son, Clarence Jr.

IRVING W. WISWALL.

Irving (1859-1937) married Effie Winne (1869-1958). He donated the "Wiswall Park" land to the village in 1910. He was one of the Presidents [Mayors] of the village. The park was intended to function as one piece, with no structures permitted on the land. Irving Wiswall made a speech at the centennial celebration in 1907.

A social club called The Saratoga club of Saratoga Springs was in Saratoga County. In 1876, the club was created, and Irving was named a trustee when it was incorporated in 1887. The club, so exclusive, restricted its membership to sixty-five, not just men.

Lanson (1864–1925) held the supervisor position for the Town of Milton once. He resided on Middle Line Road and a member of the Christ Episcopal Church. He married Ada Bateman (1870-1954). They had three children, an infant son who was stillborn, Sidney, and Alice.

In Ballston Spa, Sidney worked as a postal clerk for over forty years. He married Irene Johns (1880–1971).

Alice was born in Ballston Spa and graduated from Ballston Spa High School. She resided in Schenectady for 35 years and attended Christ Episcopal Church. She was married to Elmer Ellsworth Cooke (1887–1969).

Roscoe (1894-1973) belonged to First Presbyterian Church, Ballston Spa. He held membership in Veterans of Foreign Wars in Ballston Spa and Milton Grange. He served in the Navy in WWI, on the USS Quinebaug as a minelayer. He married Margaret Gilman (1898–1981). Together, they had one son, Roscoe.

# Legacies: Men of Quiet Impact

## *Men of Quiet Impact*

The wind is still quiet.
reflection in the sky, in the water,
Man's instinct for humanity
to be human, to be a provider
To be strong, to be a husband
To be a father, to be a man
Care for others.
The hearts of doctors, medicine men,
the intelligence of lawyers, judges,
businessmen, who cared for more.
than just the schillings in their pocket
To give, to protect, to serve
To be husband.
To be a man.
Just to make a difference
to support a family
to be alive
to be remembered.
*- Amy Shannon 2025*

# Joshua Aldridge (1766-1837)

*Husband, father, landowner, Hotel Owner*

Joshua married Priscilla Aldridge (1763–1839). He inherited property from Joseph Westcot and married Joseph's wife, Priscilla. He became proprietor of the hotel on the property, and named it, The Aldridge House. With his new wife, and his inheritance, he was able to help create new roadways for the town. As one of the leading landowners, Joshua, following the lead of Nicholas Low, ceded part of their land for these roads. Some of the early roads were Front Street, Bath Street, McMaster Street, High Street, and Milton Avenue, along with side roads.

Joshua and Priscilla had two children, Eliza, who passed just a few months after her first birthday, and Norman, who lived almost 21 years.

## *The Aldridge House: A Memory in Bloom*

Benajah Douglas built the Douglas Hotel in 1792; it was one of Ballston Spa's first and most famous hotels. Douglas was grandfather to the 1860 presidential hopeful, Stephen Douglas. Ballston Spa's emergence as a resort town was linked to its mineral springs.

After the Douglasses departed, their influence lessened, and the house was sold. Joseph Westcot, Reuben's dad, bought property in 1795, initiating a history that would merge with another family's. The house was given to Joshua Aldridge after Joseph died, who subsequently married Joseph's widow, uniting a legacy with quiet dedication.

Joshua altered the property, increasing its size and improving its landscape, resulting in a blissful summer retreat. Hidden from sun and moon, young hearts wandered for generations beneath the pines on shaded paths. In the twilight's hush, beneath the poplars and the rising moon, secrets were whispered, hands held, and vows were sealed with kisses.

The first season under his management, the house was constantly overcrowded, and Mr. Aldridge immediately built a large wing in the west, and another to the north, for a dancing hall, more than doubling the size of the house. The dance hall, after a few years, was moved across the street.

The structure on the hill stood as a silent witness to these tender exchanges, while music drifted upward from the ballroom below. Time passed, and those youthful summers faded into memory, yet many an elder, stooped by years and softened by longing, still carries the scent of pine and the echo of laughter in the chambers of the heart.

Consequently, Aldridge House survived, not as a resort, but as a place of remembrance. The beauty of it remains in memory, the laughter, and in the dignified silence of those who loved there. Once called the Aldridge House, the Brookside Museum in Saratoga County is a historical landmark with a rich past.

In 1792, Benajah Douglas built a log cabin near the spring, which was later expanded into a hotel. In 1795, Joshua Aldridge purchased the hotel, enlarged it, and named it the "Aldridge House," charging $8 per week for guests. In the early 19th Century, the house continued to be a hotel and lodging for visitors to the springs, which made Ballston Spa a popular tourist destination. In the mid-19th Century, the building was sold and used for various purposes, including a private residence, a boys' school, and apartments. In 1970, the Saratoga County Historical Society purchased the building and opened it to the public as the Brookside Museum. In 1975, the building was listed on the National Register of Historic Places.

*Aldridge House*

# Isaiah Blood (1810-1870)

Isaiah Blood shaped more than tools, he shaped a hamlet. Isaiah was a craftsman, father, husband, industrialist, patriot, and businessman. After marrying Jane Gates, he joined his father's trade and chose the forge over the storefront, taking up the scythe shop with steady hands and a visionary mind. What began as a small operation grew into Bloodville, a settlement of laborers and families nestled near Ballston Spa, where the clang of axes and scythes rang through the valley.

RESIDENCE OF THE LATE ISAIAH BLOOD, BLOODVILLE, SARATOGA Co.,N.Y.

Isaiah built a community. When fire claimed the axe works, he rebuilt, larger, stronger. When the Scythe Works fell to flame, he rose again. His tools bore the mark "I. Blood," and that name traveled far, trusted by lumbermen across the Western Hemisphere. During the Civil War, he forged battle-axes for a Massachusetts artillery company, blades shaped like short, curved swords, symbols of utility and resolve.

Besides his work at the forge, Isaiah was a member of the Assembly, State Senate, and was appointed to New York's war committee to recruit soldiers. His direction was always precise and purposeful, spanning the factory and community.

However, tradition isn't always straightforward. Isaiah's child could not carry the name forward. After his death, the business passed to a son-in-law, and for two decades, the fires of Bloodville still burned. Then came the final blaze. The factories were lost, the workers scattered, and the village named for a man of iron faded into memory.

Isaiah Blood rests in Ballston Spa Village Cemetery. His tools endure in corners, stamped with pride. His story, like so many, is a forge of beginnings and endings, echoes of labor, leadership, and loss.

Their daughter, Helen, married Henry Knickerbacker. Together, they had two children, William Hale Knickerbacker (1858–1913), and Henry Knickerbacker Jr. (1866–1888). Mrs Knickerbacker died when she jumped from the window of her apartment in New York City, on Central Park West.

Their son, William Clarence, lived only five years. He drowned in the dam of his father's scythe works factory.

Sadly, his legacy didn't last long after his death, and his children died without descendants. After Mr. Blood passed away, his son-in-law managed the business for two decades. Fire ravaged and ruined the factories. The workmen had to relocate with their families to find different jobs. The Bloodville story concluded, yet its tales persist through those familiar with it. Bloodlines don't determine the fate of legacies.

The Blood Mansion, also known as "The Maples" and later the Knickerbocker Mansion, is located on Maple Avenue in Milton, just north of Ballston Spa, within the area once known as Bloodville. It was built by Isaiah Blood in 1834, and some remnants of his industrial legacy can still be found, though the mansion is private property.

Blood Family's Final Resting Place
(one of the tallest, if not the tallest in the Ballston Spa Village Cemetery)

# Andrew Booth (1844-1921)

*Telegraph, Bank, and Memory*

Andrew Booth entered the world in Ballston Spa on December 1, 1844, the son of Wheeler Booth (1806–1877) and Charlotte Smith (1810–1882). His father, born in Galway, established himself in Ballston Spa as a successful merchant, operating a thriving mercantile business that earned him respect and prominence. Wheeler Booth's career was cut short by failing health, but his reputation endured. For forty years he was a devoted member of Christ Church, serving as vestryman until his death at 71. Charlotte was the daughter of Samuel and Lucinda Smith. She lived to see her husband's passing, but died in 1882 at 72, succumbing to congestive pneumonia.

Andrew grew up in a household marked by both promise and sorrow. His siblings included Margaret (1837–1903), Sarah (1838–1904), Samuel (1844–1863), and Mary (1847–1916).

Margaret's tragic death beneath a locomotive in Ballston Spa was widely reported and left a lasting impression on the family.

Samuel, Andrew's twin, died young during the Civil War era, a reminder of the fragility of life in that generation. These losses shaped Andrew's sense of duty and his lifelong devotion to community institutions.

Communication was transformed by the electric telegraph, a defining technology of the mid-1800s. News used to be delivered slowly through the mail, trains, or horses. This was immediately transformed by the telegraph, which relayed information quickly over long distances. As it united far-off areas and made information cheaper, it became essential for commerce, journalism, and government.

Those who operated telegraphs were seen as highly skilled professionals. Achieving mastery in Morse code required precision, speed, and focus. Operators were trusted by communities for confidential business dealings. Telegraph offices in small towns were busy places, and the operator was both a technician and information keeper.

For men like Andrew Booth, telegraphy offered entry into the professional class. It was not merely employment but a vocation that demanded technical skill and civic responsibility.

Booth's work at Western Union in the 1870s and 1880s put him at the center of this change, symbolizing the transition from old business practices to modern communication and finance.

Andrew's community involvement went beyond his work. He was a founding member of the Utopian Club, a group dedicated to conversation, culture, and civic involvement, which began in 1885. He led discussions and built community ties while serving as president for many years. His leadership reflected Ballston Spa's change from a quiet village to an industry and cultural center.

On January 11, 1889, Andrew's influence increased with his election as president of the Ballston Spa National Bank. Local banks served a purpose beyond finance. The bank, led by Booth, was key to modernizing Ballston Spa by funding local businesses and assisting residents with economic changes.

For nearly two decades, Booth was re-elected annually, a sign of the confidence placed in him by his peers and the community. His presidency coincided with a period of economic expansion, when small towns like Ballston Spa were integrating into broader financial networks. Banks were essential in channeling savings into investment, supporting railroads, mills, and local businesses. Booth's careful stewardship ensured that the institution remained both solvent and respected.

His retirement in 1907, prompted by poor health, concluded his notable service. Nevertheless, his job had already made him important in the village's money matters. He was remembered as both a banker and a civic leader, understanding finance's link to community well-being.

Andrew was also in charge of the Ballston Spa Cemetery Association, looking after the memory of the dead. He went beyond administration, embracing heritage and reminiscence. The preservation of burial grounds as places of respect and history was a key function of 19th-century civic institutions. They worked to keep cemeteries dignified, protected, and remembered.

Booth helped protect Ballston Spa's history by leading the Cemetery Association. People viewed cemeteries as museums, with each headstone sharing a story. His leadership highlighted reminiscence's importance, similar to progress. The directors showed how much they valued him by accepting his 1921 resignation "with regret".

Andrew's life was rich in fellowship and civic duty. He served as president of the Ballston Spa

Progressive Domino and Shoe Club, a social organization that blended recreation with community spirit. He sat on the committee for the Soldiers' Monument, ensuring that local veterans were honored, and he represented Milton on the Board of Supervisors, where he was remembered as a "gentleman."

His charitable acts, though modest, revealed his generosity. He contributed a dollar, joining neighbors who donated money, food, or goods to support the fair of 1905. He continued his father's tradition of service at Christ Church, where he was a vestryman, sustaining the congregation that had shaped his family's life for generations.

Andrew Booth passed away on June 6, 1921, at the age of seventy-six, in the home of his niece, Charlotte Newton. He was laid to rest in the Ballston Spa Village Cemetery, among the community he had served with constancy and care. Since he never married, his estate was divided among nieces and nephews. Valued at $2,500 in real estate and over $10,000 in personal property, his bequests included monetary gifts to Samuel Taverner and Harry Newton, and jewelry to his nieces Francis Beecher Hall and Charlotte Newton.

From the telegraph age to modern banking, Andrew Booth's life was a bridge. His dedication to camaraderie, remembrance, and community governance still shows his service commitment and community spirit.

—Saturday's Ballston *Journal* says:

Andrew Booth, of this village, for many years a telegrapher at the Ballston depot, will operate in the service of the Western Union company at Saratoga Springs, during the summer season. He is to begin next week. His experience and skill have elevated him to a proficiency attained by few.

And besides, Andrew is one of the most worthy and gentlemanly young men in his profession. And that is saying a good deal, by lightning!

### Andrew S. Booth.

Andrew S. Booth, 76, died this afternoon in the home of his niece, Miss Charlotte D. Newton, in High street Mr. Booth was born in this village, son of the late Wheeler K. Booth. He was one of the first members of the Utopian club when it was first organized in 1885 and for many years served as its president. He had held the positions of president of the Ballston Spa National bank and the Ballston Spa Cemetery association. His only survivors are nephews and nieces.

# BIG ESTATE LEFT BY ANDREW BOOTH

## Nephews and Nieces to Share Property of Late Ballston Resident.

An estate valued at $2,500, in real estate, and personal property exceeding $10,000 in value is distributed by the terms of the will of Andrew S. Booth, late of Ballston Spa., which has been admitted to probate by Surrogate W. S. Ostrander. Attached to the will is a codicil which bequeathes $2,500 to a nephew, Samuel R. Taverner of Plainfield, N. J., a former Ballstonian; $2,000 to a grand nephew, Harry H. Newton of Ballston Spa., a gold watch and chain to Mrs. Frances Beecher Hall of Ballston, and other jewelry to a niece, Charlotte B. Newton, of Ballston.

Samuel S. Newton of Ballston, a nephew, who is the executor of the instrument, and Charlotte B. Newton are named as residuary legatees.

### Wagner Will Probated.

The will of Augusta A. Wagner, late of Saratoga Srings, leaving an estate of $2,400 to a daughter, Fanny A. C. Berger of Schenectady, has been admitted to probate by Surrogate Ostrander. Miss Berger has been granted letters testamentary.

# James Comstock (1786-1851)

James Comstock was born in Massachusetts, to Jeremiah Comstock and Hannah Butterworth Bowen, who were married in 1772. James had eight siblings, Jeremiah, Samuel, Anna, Elizabeth, Joseph, Benjamin, and Jesse.

James arrived in Ballston Spa in 1803 and soon became a local leader. He bought The Independent American in 1811, moving its printing office from Court House Hill to Ballston Spa. For thirty-five years, editor Comstock promoted Whig principles with conviction, recognized as a strong individual and community leader.

His ownership of the newspaper extended to the printing office, through which he published numerous works, including *Lectures on the Prophecies* and *The Three Woe-Trumpets* by Elhanan Winchester. In 1814, he printed the first Temperance tract ever published in New York State. The press remained active until its sale to J. O. Nodyne in 1847.

James' bookstore had a reading room, and he also did editorial work there. He was among the first trustees of the new church in Ballston Spa in 1834. He kept contributing, becoming postmaster in 1849, a role he alone was chosen for.

James was married to Mary Sears (1786–1869). He died on July 26, 1851, at seventy, leaving behind a legacy of print, principle, and reticent leadership.

James and Mary, united by faith, spent decades together in Ballston Spa. They were married in 1813. She observed the village's initial printing press, the establishment of its Presbyterian church, and the widening reach of Temperance ideals, which she embraced with dignity and certainty.

Though history speaks more loudly of her husband's public deeds, Mary's legacy rests in the spirit of partnership, in the moral compass she helped shape, and in the home, she tended with care. She lived to see the village grow, the press changed hands, and the seeds of reform take root.

Mary is buried in Ballston Spa Village Cemetery, her life a gentle reflection of faith, resilience, and shared purpose.

This QR code is the direct link to the first printed books in Ballston on Essence Enterprises' website.

# William Child (1777-1840)

William Child was born in 1777 to Increase Child (1740–1810) and Olive Pease (1736–1822). In 1798, he married Mary Reed (1777–1847), and together they raised nine children: Janette, William, Mary, George, John, Faber, Mark, Stanley, and Harriet.

William was essential to the creation of the region's first newspapers. The Saratoga Register or Farmers' Journal, the county's first newspaper, was printed in 1798 by Increase Child and his father at Court House Hill in Ballston. As stated on its title page, the publication office was above Messrs. Robert Leonard & Co.'s store, which was almost across from the Court House. Known as The Journal, it aided the administration of John Adams and his political group. Despite being small, four pages, and lacking local news, it started printing media in Saratoga County. Writing was clearly his passion, and he had a suitable way to express it.

From 1808 to 1818, William Child published the *Ballston Gazette*, the first abiding newspaper in the county. Printed by Child and issued by various publishers, including Comstock & Bates, the Gazette was a weekly newspaper that offered updates on local events, politics, and society. It became a cornerstone of community discourse and a reflection of Ballston Spa's cultural and civic life.

In 1810, following the disbandment of his publishing partnership, William assumed sole management of the business.

William's legacy in Ballston Spa endures as a testament to the power of written media in fostering community, dialogue, and historical record. His early efforts laid the foundation for journalism in Saratoga County. The original *Saratoga Register* evolved over time and is now known as the *Ballston Journal*, originally published by H. L. Grose & Sons.

# JS L'Amoreaux 1837-1918

Born to Jesse and Charity L'Amoreaux, Jesse was the only son among sisters Elizabeth, Catherine, and Sarah. He entered the legal world early, opening his first practice in Schuylerville before settling in Ballston Spa, a village then rising with industry and reputation.

Jesse became a pillar of the community. He helped organize the First National Bank of Ballston

Spa, serving as director, vice-president, and eventually president. His legal career spanned decades, from high-profile criminal cases to corporate counsel, and he partnered with Hon. George Graham in New York City. In 1882, he was elected judge of Saratoga County without opposition, serving until 1887.

Being in Ballston Spa's core, he was in the Masonic order and a long-time First Presbyterian Church member. Saratoga County, an Historical Address, was published by him in 1876, recording the area's past. Later, he invested in property in

**"Cuts" Him in Good Shape.**
The Albany *Express* in its weekly edition, issued to-day, presents a fine two-column cut and an appreciative personal sketch of Judge Jesse S. L'Amoreaux, of Ballston Spa, the Republican candidate for comptroller. The *Express* says that "Judge L'Amoreaux will make one of the best comptrollers the state has had in many a year."

Saratoga Springs, a lingering reminder of the village's waning rivalry with its more famous neighbor.

Jesse married Ellen Holbrook, but they had no children. Though Ballston Spa's renown as a tourist destination waned, Jesse's contribution marked its golden age, when the mills murmured along Kayaderosseras Creek and civic pride ran deep.

He had no direct family, but his work remains in historical records, the courthouse, and the honorable life he led.

Jessie L'Amoreaux's Final Resting Place

# Captain William McKittrick (1829–1864)

Before war called him to the front, William McKittrick worked in the Saratoga County Clerk's office and may have stitched lives together as a merchant tailor in Ballston Spa. He married Caroline Holmes, and together they had two children: William and Mary. Their son would later ride westward, becoming a cattle rancher in California.

When the Civil War began, he volunteered without hesitation, rising to lead Company C of the 115th Regiment, New York Volunteers.

He died in action at Fort Gilmer, Virginia, on September 29, 1864, during a charge. His bravery and death are remembered by his friends and the public. McKittrick's life of service was rooted in both community and faith, as a Mason and Episcopalian.

In 1875, the Grand Army of the Republic honored Captain McKittrick by naming Post No. 46 after him. The G.A.R. circle in Ballston Spa Village Cemetery stands as a tribute to the veterans who followed his path.

His son, bearing the same name, continued the legacy of service, joining the staff of Major-General Shafter in California during later military campaigns.

CAPTAIN WILLIAM H. McKITTRICK.

Captain McKittrick's story is one of devotion and sacrifice. Though his life was cut short, his name enduring stone, in memory, and in the circle where veterans rest.

# Dr. Leverett Moore (1805–1892)

## *Farmer, Student, Doctor, Counselor, Investor*

Born to John and Nancy Moore, Leverett came from sturdy New England roots. Orphaned at seven, he was placed with a local farmer, where he worked the fields in the summers and studied in the winters. With little more than determination and a hunger for learning, he taught school to fund his education, eventually pursuing classical studies in Granville, Massachusetts.

At 21, he turned to medicine. He completed his training, and began a modest practice in Ulster County, then moved to Albany, and later to Greenbush, where his reputation grew.

He resided in Ballston Spa starting in 1840. Dr. Moore served the village with excellence for over thirty years.

Aside from his medical profession, he participated in the Saratoga County Medical Society and the Union Medical Association. Despite his Republican views, he chose not to run for office, preferring to serve by helping people. He was also an investor in local industry, including oil cloth manufacturing, the gas works, and the National Bank of Ballston Spa, where he was a director and vice-president.

At 71, Dr. Moore retired, his life characterized by stable work and quiet success. In 1892, he passed away peacefully, remembered for his service and sincerity. His first marriage was to Elizabeth Allen of Albany, and they had three children. He married Mary Smith of Ballston Spa after she died. His daughter, Mary Moore, and her stepmother continued to live in their home on Milton Avenue, a place of comfort and remembrance.

Dr. Moore's life was not one of spectacle, but of unwavering devotion, to healing, to family, and to the village he called home.

DR. MOORE.

The above pictures of the home of the late Dr. Leverett Moore and of himself will be gladly received by his many friends and readers of the Ballston Journal, to whom his memory is almost sacred. The home is still occupied by his widow, Mrs. Mary L. (Smith) Moore, and his only daughter, Miss Mary R. Moore, and to them it is made sacred by the fond memories of the days when husband and father was with them.

Leverett Moore, M. D., was in every sense a self-made man. Left an orphan at the age of seven years, he worked his way unaided to the exceptionally high position he reached in his profession and in society.

Dr. Moore was born at Palmer, Mass., December 9, 1805. He was the son of John and Nancy (Gibson) Moore. His father died when he was only seven years old, and he was placed with a farmer in the vicinity of his home to be reared and educated, working summers and attending school winters. How he improved his time may be seen from the fact that at the age of eighteen he began teaching school. By this means he worked his way through a classical school at Granville, Mass. At twenty-one years of age he began reading medicine, and in December, 1829, graduated from the medical college of Pittsfield, Mass.

He began practice in Ulster county, N. Y., but after a short time moved to Albany, where he remained until September, 1834, when he changed his office to Greenbush, opposite Albany.

In 1840 Dr. Moore made Ballston Spa his home, where he lived respected and beloved until his death, which occurred July 13, 1892.

Besides his practice as a physician, and attention to his duties as a member of the Saratoga County Medical Association and of the Union Medical Association of Washington, Warren and Saratoga counties, the doctor became interested in manufacturing, and was for several years a member of the firm of Wakeman, Wait & Co., oil cloth manufacturers. He was a director for many years of the Ballston Spa, afterward the Ballston Spa National Bank.

Although he retired from active practice at the age of 71 years, yet his patrons almost obliged him to care for them in times of sickness for many years. He lived to the ripe old age of nearly eighty-seven years to enjoy the large competency he had acquired.

RESIDENCE OF MRS. LEVERETT MOORE.

*Final resting place of Dr. Leverett
Moore*

# Colonel Samuel Young (1779-1850)

The Youngs' family was known for its reserved strength, love of learning, and faith. In Ballston Spa, they began building their tradition of knowledge and guidance. Samuel Young, their most distinguished leader, exemplified family values, work ethic, education, and community service. Through the use of law, politics, and education, the Youngs helped their community's character develop through the years.

Colonel Samuel Young (1779-1850), the son of Thomas and Anna Young, was born in Massachusetts. He was the second of the brood, the initial son, which comprised siblings Rachel, Lucinda, and Clarinda. The Youngs moved from Stamford, Connecticut, to Ballston Spa, where they settled on a farm, the place that shaped Samuel's character and future.

Even with limited formal schooling at the district school, Samuel's desire to learn never went away. He stabilized farm labor with study, often reading late into the night by the glow of a pine knot.

Samuel was a law student of Judge Emott and developed a busy law practice. Following his marriage to Mary Gibson, he bought a farm on Academy Hill and constructed his house and law office there. Mary and Samuel were parents to seven children: John, Catharine Ann, Samuel Jr., Thomas Gibson, Louisa, Mary, and Charlotte.

After Mary died, Samuel wed Sarah Barns in 1826. They had five children, Margaret, Jane, Lucinda, Thomas, and Clarinda, names that echoed the legacy of Samuel's sisters and forebears.

Samuel's public life was marked by service and esteem. His roles included Ballston supervisor, Assembly speaker, New York canal commissioner, and militia colonel. Though he ran for governor in 1824, DeWitt Clinton won instead. After being appointed judge by Governor Marcy, he took over from Judge Thompson.

Samuel continued to study after retiring, focusing on classical, scientific, and legal fields. He was a member of the Masonic Lodge and served as an officer for the Saratoga County Bible Society. He moved to his farm north of Academy Hill in 1847 and kept on reading, thinking, and serving.

Samuel Young, a self-made man of 71, left his mark on Ballston Spa and beyond through his discipline and intellectual curiosity.

The final resting place of Samuel Young

# The Steady Flame: Hands of a Village

## *The steady flame*

With spirit and faith
a love for the calloused hands
the scent of cedar, pine, oak
the gentle push of the wood plane
The gloss of the paint brushed.
across the canvas, on the wall
The gripping internal love
to build, to create, to sustain
to craft, to have a trade.
Something that builds up.
and tears down
not for bad, but for
something new
The wood chips dropping to the ground.
the splatter of sweat, wiping a brow.
dedication, imagination
a quiet legacy left behind.
More than a footnote
Higher than a lantern's flame,
quieter than a feather falling from the sky.
For the love of family
For the love of community
to keep the flame of creativity, flickering
-Amy Shannon 2025

Not everyone is listed as "notable." Have you ever strolled through a cemetery, taking care to look at each of the stones, wondering about the person who once lived, now who lies under that stone? I can't stroll, but I used to. Now, I roll (I have a wheelchair), and go where I can, when I can, but wherever there is a stone, there is a story. I noticed on some stones, there is a short story about the person, even if it is something simple as "wife of," or some relation. Sometimes, the wife was buried, but listed under her maiden name, and then it would say "wife of…" Now, we get names and dates, and sometimes a note like "loving mother," "loving father," and such. Some men get something so prominent as a scripture or their family motto, bringing another part of their story to share above ground.

As I took to the cemeteries, I found stones that called to me, not in a ghostly way (though, I believe in spirits), just pulling me toward them, asking me to tell their story, so I made a note of the stones, took photos, and went through my videos for hours to see if there was something I missed. Then, I looked into the person's history, their story, and that is where this chapter leads. I noticed their names because I was brought to their stone. You can tell a lot about a person's life by their gravestone, monument, headstone, simple or extravagant, and of course, their obituary. Sometimes, you must sit quietly and listen, and they will share their story, and it's my job to tell it.

# The Bathricks

## *Stewards of craft, kinship, and civic care*

Arthur Bathrick (1865–1940), born in 1865 to Obadiah Bathrick and Polly Felts, came from a family deeply connected to Saratoga County's working soil. He wed Florence Hayes, daughter of Elias and Margaret Hayes, in 1886. Devoted to family, craft, and community, Arthur and Florence built a life with their son, Raymond Arthur.

Though seldom mentioned, Arthur's influence is evident everywhere. The tradesman was a painter at General Electric, mixing factory work with art. With his hands, he built dwellings, messages, and possibly the walls that observed a century's evolution.

However, Arthur's influence wasn't just physical. His career in public service began in 1907 when he cast his ballot. Despite the lack of clarity, records hint he was a Democrat on a town board or committee in Malta or Ballston Spa. He belonged to the Maccabees and Odd Fellows, groups showing his dedication to helping others.

Florence (1869-1949) was one of five children. Her siblings, Nelson, Ophelia, William, and Francis, were raised with her in Clifton Park, where the Hayes family were pioneers. Florence lived through massive change, from horses to cars, letters to radio. In every situation, she was constant, grounding her family with dignity and fortitude.

Together, Arthur and Florence weathered the seasons of life. Their shared monument at Dunning Street Cemetery in Malta stands as a testament to their enduring bond. Arthur, the craftsman and citizen; Florence, was the cherished daughter of pioneers and matriarch of memory. In life, they built and nurtured. In rest, they remain rooted in the land they helped shape, where the colors of memory never fade.

Raymond (1898–1965) was born in Burnt Hills. He carried the legacy of his parents into a life of faith, service and true devotion. In 1919, he married Gladys Sigsbee Whitmyre, and later, he shared his days with Doris Taylor Bathrick. Though the records speak softly, they trace a life ingrained in work, worship, and community.

Raymond spent 43 years with General Electric's grounds and building department in Schenectady, shaping the spaces others passed through daily. His long tenure earned him membership in the GE Quarter Century Club, a badge of endurance and dedication.

He and his wife were active members of Sacred Heart Church, where Raymond lent his basso voice to the choir, filling the sanctuary with low, resonant harmony. In Alplaus, Doris welcomed guests to her home as part of the "hooked rug" group, a social circle that stitched together stories and companionship.

Raymond's final resting place is in the Bathrick family plot at Dunning Street Cemetery in Malta, where generations of quiet service and civic care lie beneath the soil. His life, like his father's, was painted in steady strokes, on grounds, in song, and through the rituals of community.

Though the records leave questions about transitions, about Doris's fuller story, they leave echoes. In the choir's harmony, in the church's pews, in the rugs laid out for guests, Raymond's presence lingers. Not loud, but lasting.

# The Fords

John S "Bona" (1800-1888) was born in Ballston Spa, NY in 1800. He was born before the village was incorporated in 1807. He

married Roxanna Stone (1803–1837), and together they had at least four children. Elizabeth, William, John Benjamin and Hiram. He was the owner of a bowling alley for forty years, and it was a popular spot for bowling enthusiasts. He served as constable of Ballston Spa, and was a village Trustee. Roxanna, his first wife, passed away in 1837. Mary Jane Bridges became his wife in 1878, his second marriage. He was the oldest Ballston Spa resident at his passing, having lived there his entire life. He was almost 88 when he died. According to his obituary, he was the father of seven children.

**OCTOGENARIAN FORD.**

Lived Nearly Eighty-Eight Years in Ballston—A Widely Known Citizen Passed Away.

John S. Ford, widely known as "Bona" Ford, a brief notice of whose death appeared in yesterday's SARATOGIAN, was regarded as Ballston's "oldest inhabitant." He was born in this village on February 12th, in the year 1800 and lacked just one month of being 88 years old and has resided here all his life. For forty years he kept a bowling alley where the stores of Moses Lewis and Charles Massey now stand, which became famous as a resort for sporting men and others. He once served as town constable and village trustee. He was twice married. His first wife was Miss Roxina Stone, by whom he had seven children, three daughters, Marion, Rebecca and Elizabeth, all deceased, and four sons, Benjamin, William, Sanborn and Hiram, the latter two now deceased, and the two former still being residents of this place. He is survived by his second wife, who was Miss Mary Jane Bridges, whom he married 15 years ago.

Rebecca (1826-) married Sylvester Davis (1823-1860). There are very limited records on Rebecca, and it is unknown if they had any children.

John (1829–1905) served in the Union Army during the American Civil War, in Company D of the 4th NY Heavy Artillery. He wed Sarah J Ferris Ford (1828–1908). Frank (1855-1944), their son, lived a long life after he matured, wed and had offspring. John served as a constable in Malta. He also helped establish the police force in the town of Milton. Constables held elected positions back then. John's career took him from constable in Malta to Milton's elected official. John's career path led him to become a deputy sheriff.

There is an article about John and sailing under an article's head "A Deputy Sheriff Takes A Bath." He learned the he didn't like sailing when his sailboat capsized on Saratoga Lake. John was an auctioneer. In 1880, John was appointed as "special deputy sheriffs for criminal business." One article in the news archives mentions that he was part of a murder investigation. John was a "famous" deputy in the eyes of his community.

William (1827-) married Melissa Elizabeth, and they had at least two children, John S Ford, and William Ford II. There are only a few mentions of William Ford in any record, such as his father's obituary, and his brother, Hiram's obituary. He was his Hiram's business partner for a while.

Hiram (1832–1877) was born in Ballston Spa. He married Mary Ann Tripp, and they had at least seven children, some being identified as Mariam, George, Ettie, and Lorella. He was a slight man, with a very slender body. He had a good mind for business. He and his brother, William, were in business together for 18 years, and both had gained property. Hiram owned a ranch in Colorado and was an extensive cattle ranchman. He had some business troubles, and slanderous falsehood reports, and this affected him greatly, both physically and mentally. He was part of mining camps, as a speculator, and those who knew him, knew the side of him that had a kind heart, he was a generous friend to many. "Green be the sod above thee. Friend of my better days. None knew thee but to love thee. Nor love thee but to praise."

Frances "Elizabeth" (1834–1835) lived almost one year, leaving behind her memory and her empty crib.

The Fords Final Resting Place

# The Hides

Samuel Hides (1806-1888) originated in England. The farmer's farm was on Ballston Street, right by the village cemetery. Reverend Father Peter Haverman bought a plot from Samuel Hides to enlarge the Ballston Spa Village Cemetery's graveyard. The legacy says it was bought in 1840. The rites of the church were used by Reverend Haverman to consecrate the ground. Land donations and purchases shaped the current village cemetery. Samuel and Mary Elizabeth became parents to five children after they wed. Samuel had three wives, but the third one didn't last. Samuel was a valuable man who also directed the Ballston Spa National Bank.

Samuel was a "black and white smith," and opened a shop he called for "general Smithy business" and was fully equipped to perform such tasks.

Samuel was a spiritualist and was part of the spiritualist society. Samuel discovered what he referred to as the Franklin springs. In 1868, Samuel Hides was living on Malta Avenue and believed in mediums and having seances. He believed that he communicated with the spirit of Benjamin Franklin, who told him where to find a spring that would have medicinal value. Hides followed Franklin's instructions. In April 1869, after drilling through earth and rock to a depth of

*A MARRIAGE ANNULLED.*

Troy, Feb. 14.—In 1880 Samuel Hides, age seventy-seven, a wealthy resident of Ballston Spa, was induced by a clairvoyant known as Mrs. Dr. Mann to marry her upon her representing that the spirits had so ordered it. Hides was a firm believer in spiritualism, and acting under the supposed advice of spirits he at once dug for a mineral spring at Ballston, and found it 715 feet below the surface. It is now valued at $25,000. He consented to the marriage, and made a deed at her request, it is alleged, conveying the spring property to her. A short time after this Hides began an action to annul the marriage and set aside the conveyance, on the ground that he had been imposed upon. Judge Waite, the referee, to-day decided in favor of Hides.

seven hundred and fifteen feet, the water came rushing up with great velocity and was thrown into the air more than fifty feet. The Franklin Spring was found.

In 1880, Samuel and Mary's court case was reported on in news articles. Samuel believed Mary, a self-declared psychic, had put a spell on him to marry her and get his wealth.

Mary Elizabeth (1821–1858) was his first wife, and mother of Samuel's children. She died before her young children died, and yes, she was still young at 37 with a lifetime ahead of her.

Samuel Jr (1842–1859) lived only seventeen years. He died in his sleep after lingering illness, his story carried forward in reminiscence.

Mary (1845–1864) was staying in New York City at the Merchant's Hotel and died of consumption at 19 years of age.

Susan Adelaide (1850–1912) married Abijah Comstock in 1869. They had a son in 1877, Walter Hides Comstock, who moved to Los Angeles, California, where he married and had children of his own.

Louise (1852–1869) lived but seventeen years. A long illness silenced her days, yet she is remembered in love.

Grace "Gracie" (1857–1868) lived almost eleven years, her brief life remembered in light and love.

# Arnold Phineas Jones (1854–1932)

Arnold Phineas Jones's parents, Joseph Stafford Jones and Eunice Etta Lewis, gave birth to him in Round Lake. In 1879, he and Jennie Louise Black were married. The four children were Howard Douglas, Grace Blanche, Floyd Leroy and Clifford Leon "Cliff" Jones. Following the passing of Jennie Louise, his wife, he relocated westward with their four kids. He was a resident of Anthony, Minnesota in 1900, and afterward, he and his offspring moved to King, Washington. He wed Mary "Alice" Black, Jennie's older sister, in 1893. Arnold was assisted by Alice Black in raising her sister's kids. Jennie was buried in Dunning Cemetery in Malta, NY, and has a large monument. The monument also has her husband's name on it, without a date. The gravestone is an exact replica of her sister Mary Alice & Arnold's in the Evergreen Cemetery in Enumclaw, Washington. It stood for a long time until it was requested that it lay down in the ground.

Migration, resilience, and family love define Arnold's narrative. Jennie's death caused him such grief that he desired to leave. He required support in bringing up his offspring. After Jennie's death, his move west showed the era's search for healing and opportunity. His marriage to Mary Alice, Jennie's sister, suggests a wish to uphold family ties and ensure stability for his kids. A quiet pioneer, he settled on government land, raised a family in Washington, and carried memories of Saratoga County after receiving free land.

He died on 10 December 1932, in Auburn, King, Washington, America, at 78. He is buried with his second wife, Mary Alice Black.

# The Pitts

Louisa West (1828–1894) was born to George West and Jane Blackmore West in 1828. She is the sister of Elizabeth West Mortimore, George West, and Martha West Brown. Her brother, George was the "paper bag King." Louisa married James Pitts (1828–1874) and they had two children, James Jr, and Ada. The Wests were a prominent family in Ballston Spa, due to the success of George West.

James (1828-1874) was a veteran. He served in Co. K 146 Regiment NYS Vol. (Company K, 146th Regiment New York State Volunteers) This military unit was an infantry regiment that served in the Union Army during the American Civil War from October 1862 to July 1865. The regiment was raised and organized in Rome, NY, and was known by several nicknames. They participated in many major battles, including Fredericksburg, Chancellorsville, Gettysburg, the Wilderness, and the Siege of Petersburg, and were known for their distinctive Zouave-style uniforms (It generally included short open-fronted jackets, baggy trousers, sashes, and a fez-like chéchia head-dress). James died 20 years before his wife. They are buried together in the Ballston Spa Village Cemetery.

James Jr. (1852–1890) was named after his father. He married Fannie Birch in 1882. They had two children, Hattie and Ada Mae, who was named after her paternal aunt.

Ada (1858–1928) married Nelson F Pitts. Together, they had at least four children; Curtis, Nelson, Harry, and Charles and a daughter referred to as "Mrs. Collamer". Nelson worked at the West Paper Manufacturing business. His mother-in-law was George's sister. He was one of the oldest members of the Franklin Lodge. It is not quite clear how Ada Pitts and Nelson were related prior to getting married. Curtis was part of the Board of Education in the Corinth Union School District. Charles was one of the Corinth village presidents (1893), and one of the town clerks. There was a note that Charles was also on a jury of a very important case, Arthur McQuade, an alderman of New York City was placed on trial on the charge of having received money from the Broadway Surface Railway company of New York in consideration for voting to grant a franchise to that company.

The Pitts' final resting place

# The Relyeas

*Faith, Family, Charitable, Warmth and Dignity.*

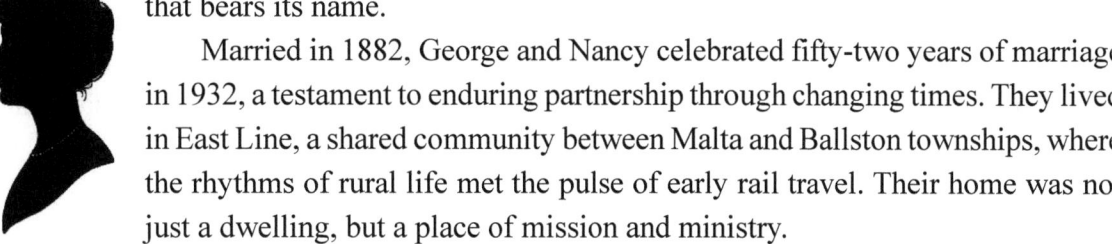

George (1856–1932) and Nancy (1861–1936) Relyea rest together at Dunning Street Cemetery in Malta, NY, their lives quietly etched into the soil of East Line, a hamlet once vibrant with railroads and meeting houses, now remembered mostly by the road that bears its name.

Married in 1882, George and Nancy celebrated fifty-two years of marriage in 1932, a testament to enduring partnership through changing times. They lived in East Line, a shared community between Malta and Ballston townships, where the rhythms of rural life met the pulse of early rail travel. Their home was not just a dwelling, but a place of mission and ministry.

The Relyeas were active missionaries for St. John's Episcopal Church. Nancy served as president of the church's Women's Auxiliary. During the Great Depression, she and her fellow volunteers prepared a "mission box" of clothing for a Virgin Islands congregation, timed for Easter. They served supper to employees of the Schenectady Savings Bank in the parish hall, a gesture of warmth and dignity in a time of national hardship.

George and Nancy had at least two children: Walter Relyea, who appears in local records and cemetery listings, and a daughter known only as Mrs. Roy Hoag. Her given name remains elusive, but her presence is felt through marriage and community ties. The family's connections extended to Henry Relyea, who frequently visited and shared familial bonds, perhaps a cousin or uncle, though the precise lineage is still being traced.

East Line Hamlet, nestled at the crossroads of Eastline Road and NY-67, was more than a dot on the map, it was a living, breathing community whose rhythms were faithfully recorded in the local press. In the early 1930s, newspaper columns regularly noted the comings and goings of its residents, from church suppers to family visits. These snippets, often just a few lines long, served as a social ledger, preserving the memory of everyday life.

George Relyea himself appeared in such mentions. In November 1932, the *Ballston Journal* reported that he had been hospitalized, a quiet signal of his declining health in the final year of his life. Though no obituary has yet surfaced, this small notice stands as a testament to the community's attentiveness and care.

The hamlet's importance went beyond its physical size. In 1809, East Line built a meeting house, which became a railroad stop by 1837. These landmarks united the community, acting as a common ground for Malta and Ballston. Though the hamlet was renamed East Line Road, its past lived on in memory and history.

George and Nancy's legacy is one of modest service, love, and roots in a place that once bustled with early American life. In remembering them, we remember East Line itself, a hamlet of small kindnesses, where the ledger of daily life was written in supper menus, mission boxes, and the gentle presence of neighbors.

The final resting place of the Relyeas

# Passage: Cradles of Memory

*A tribute to brief lives, held in love and remembered in silence.*

*Oh, to be held in mother's arms*
*to reach up and touch father's beard*
*to have a moment, a breath*

*Oh, to not be sick*
*to not see mother cry*
*nor father, turn away in grief.*

*Oh, to be loved*
*in mother's tears*
*in father's sighs*

*Oh, to be remembered*
*in mother's footsteps*
*in father's legend*

*Oh, to be something*
*other than a whisper, a whimper*
*an echo of a life unlived.*
*-Amy Shannon 2025*

# Reminiscence

Heartbroken mothers continued their responsibilities while grieving, frequently naming later children after those they'd lost, occasionally using the same name. These children are part of their families' legacy, and should be remembered, if only in faith, heart, and soul. I honor those who lost children, some before they even drew breath. I praise the mothers who kept going, keeping their grief in their hearts, but still moved forward, providing for family. When a child's name includes a bracket with a 1 or 2 inside, it signifies that the child's name had been used by another child who died.

Women faced the risk of death during childbirth in the 1700s, 1800s, and early 1900s. She could live while her child perished, or her child lived, but she didn't. Sometimes, a cough would become whooping cough, a rash would appear with fever, or the throat would be blocked by diphtheria. Scarlet fever, measles, consumption, cholera, influenza, each name a tolling bell in the households of families, who watched helplessly as their child passed.

 Eliza Aldridge, daughter of Priscilla Hewitt Aldridge and Joseph Westcot. Eliza, being nearly 1-year-old, passed before memory could grow, her name remains, a first blossom in the family's garden of reminiscence. A single daughter, held for a fleeting year, her memory quietly woven into the Aldridge and Westcot lineage.

 Malvina, only 8 years old, a child of wonder, departed before her ninth spring. She was the cherished daughter of Sarah Jane and William Beattie.

 Elizabeth, only 17 years old, was a young woman nearing adulthood. Her dreams linger in the folds of time, her name spoken with tenderness. She was the cherished daughter of Sarah Jane and William Beattie.

 Julia, only 14 years old, absence came too soon; her memory held in every shared glance. She was the cherished daughter of Sarah Jane and William Beattie.

 Cornelia, only 18 years old, touched many lives; her loss etched deeply in the family's hearts. She was the cherished daughter of Sarah Jane and William Beattie.

 William, only 17 years old, lives on in the stories passed down, his name a quiet echo in legacy. He was the beloved son of Sarah Jane and William Beattie.

 John, only 3 months old, a cherished life, a tender season, with three months of quiet wonder held close in the arms of love. He was the cherished infant son of Frances and Callender Beecher

 William Clarence, only 5 years old, a young boy's mirth had once rung out across the factory grounds, and now it traveled in the flow of each creek. He lived in the hearts of his parents, Isaiah and Jane Blood.

 Elizabeth, only 15 years old, possessed a voice that once filled the parlor, now recalled in quiet corners. She was the cherished daughter of Lucretia and Lebbeus Booth.

 Young John Chester, only 6 years old, a boy of giggles and mischief, left a hush where joy once danced. He was the beloved son of Lucretia and Lebbeus Booth.

 Martha, only 3 months old, experienced cradling for a season, love for a lifetime. She was the precious infant daughter of Lucretia and Lebbeus Booth.

 Mary Lucretia [1], only 1-year-old, a gentle bloom that departed too soon, her name carrying her mother's grace. She was the cherished daughter of Lucretia and Lebbeus Booth.

 Mary [2], only 1-year-old, was a brief light mirrored the one before her. She was the precious infant daughter of Lucretia and Lebbeus Booth.

 Isabella Graham, only 17 years old, name echoes with strength and sorrow. She was the young, endeared daughter of Lucretia and Lebbeus Booth.

 Josiah Quincy, only 8 months old, a handsewn quilt draped in the empty cradle yet love holds firm. He was the cherished infant son of Lucretia and Lebbeus Booth.

 Martha "Mattie," only 7 years old, a child of laughter and lullabies, claimed by diphtheria in her sleep. Her absence left a quiet ache in the home; her memory tucked into every folded quilt and whispered prayer. She was the adored daughter of Margaret and John Chester Booth.

 Horace, only one month old, departed, leaving behind a gentle sorrow, a cradle silenced too early under the caring gaze of loved ones. He was the cherished infant son of Mary and Nathaniel Clark.

 Joel Lee, only 2 years old, brought joy in small footsteps; his glee sent a balm to hearts still healing. He was the beloved son of Mary and Nathaniel Clark.

 Elizabeth lived less than a year, but her name endures like a whispered lullaby, soft and sacred in the hush of reminiscence. She was the cherished daughter of Mary and Nathaniel Clark.

 Charles, only 17 years old, a son of promise, departed in youth. His name still reflects the family's story; his absence is felt in every quiet moment. A young man born into the Curtiss family, leaving his own legacy.

 M. Addie, only 17 years old, touched many lives, her memory held close to the hearts of those who knew her. A young daughter, born into the Curtiss family.

 George, only 9 months old, a baby boy, whose time on Earth was limited, his memory in every cradle-rock and gentle sigh. An adored infant son born into the Curtiss family.

 Libbie, 5 years old, was a child of laughter and light. A daughter born into the Curtiss family.

 Daniel, 3 years old, a child of legacy, vanished before recollection could be established. His name remained, even as his voice fell silent. The adored young son of Martha Custis Washington and Daniel Custis.

Frances, 3 years old, was a tender blossom in the Custis garden. Her laughter once danced through the halls, now carried in echoes. She was the cherished daughter of Martha Custis Washington and Daniel Custis.

 Martha, only 17 years old, proved a young woman of promise, lost before her full bloom. Her presence shaped her mother's path; her absence left a quiet ache. A daughter, almost living to adulthood. She was the adored daughter of Martha Custis Washington and Daniel Custis.

 Jane Ann, 13 years old, was a young girl with tender years and growing promise. Her name still lingers in the hush of reminiscence, like a candle quietly burning. She was the cherished daughter of Hester and Ulysses Freeman Doubleday.

 Michael, almost 2 years old, came like spring rain; soft, brief, and full of promise. But the cradle closed before his voice could rise before his feet could chase the morning light. He was the beloved son of Sally and Richard Dunning.

 Charley, only 18 years old, offered a glimpse of potential; smallpox came like a shadow at dusk, and he slipped away. He was the beloved son of Phebe and Captain Ephraim Ellsworth.

 Ellen Jane, 11 years old, danced in the hush of girlhood grace. She was the cherished daughter of Susan and Horace Ellsworth.

Henry Elijah, only 14 years old, carried the quiet strength of his father's name. He was the beloved son of Susan and Horace Ellsworth.

 Sarah Jane and Lorenzo Ellsworth lost two daughters. Lucy Ellsworth and Dillie Belle Ellsworth. Born together, they bloomed like twin violets in spring, but the seasons turned too swiftly. Lucy was the first to pass away, her laughter silenced at four. Dillie Belle followed two years later, her small hands still reaching for the light.

 Frances "Elizabeth" only lived less than a year, a young daughter, taken before she could speak her first words, but always unforgettable, with her sweetness and soft infant scent, which lingers in the echoes of her life. She was the cherished daughter of John and Roxanna Ford.

 Jonathan Fox, only 6 years old, giggles once filled the fields, now carried in the wind that moves through memory. He was the beloved son of Rachel and Asa Fox.

 Thomas, only 8 years old, had a brother, a companion, a gentle soul. His presence remains in every family tale. He was the beloved son of Rachel and Asa Fox.

 Emily was born into silence, held in love. She was the precious infant daughter of Rachel and Asa Fox.

Alexander, only 9 years old, footsteps once echoed through the Gordon home, now carried in the hush of remembrance, where his name still stirs the heart. He was the beloved son of James and Mary Gordon.

Samuel Jr, 17 years old, a young man at his peak, his father's beloved, sharing his name; however, he experienced epilepsy, which separated him from his family prematurely. He died a year after his mother. He was the beloved son of Samuel and Mary Elizabeth Hides.

Louise, 17 years old, seemed a wondrous young woman, with a grand spirit for life, even if her life ended because of consumption (tuberculosis), and her memory remained in the heart of her family. She was the cherished daughter of Samuel and Mary Elizabeth Hides.

Grace "Gracie," only 11 years old, quiet steps of a young woman, growing up so fast, but with grace and joy, taken away too young, no chance to be a woman, but enough to leave a lingering whisper in her parent's hearts. She was the cherished daughter of Samuel and Mary Elizabeth Hides.

Angie Hollister, only 1-year-old, left behind the warmth of lullabies and the ache of arms that still remember her weight. She was the precious infant daughter of Elizabeth and Asa Hollister.

Zilpha Hollister, only 4 years old, proved to be short, but she is still a bright light that speaks to the family's experience, a name recalled with both sadness and affection. She was the cherished daughter of Elizabeth and Asa Hollister.

Young William, only 6 years old, had wide eyes and wonder; his memory lingers in the corners of the homestead. He was the beloved son of Sally Taylor and Daniel Holmes.

James Leander, only 2 years old, his laughs barely begun, now carried in the hush of family lore. He was the beloved son of Sally Taylor and Daniel Holmes.

Lucy Jane, only 14 years old, absence left a quiet ache, her name still spoken in soft remembrance. She was the cherished daughter of Sally Taylor and Daniel Holmes.

Davis, only 1-year-old, a brief illumination, kept near for a single period of the seasons prior to a return to stillness. His brief life left a quiet grace behind; a cradle memory wrapped in love and longing. He was the beloved son of Hester and Joshua Loomis.

Infant Low lived less than a year, had no name, although love existed. This initial child seemed ephemeral at the beginning. Loved infant child of Johanna and Cornelius Low.

John, under 1-years-old, life became a fleeting breath, a tender faith that never got old. Despite the brevity of his life, his name lasts like a quiet plea whispered through time. He was the cherished infant son of Johanna and Cornelius Low.

 Johanna, 6 years old, namesake of her mother, brought six years of light and love to the home. She was the cherished daughter of Johanna and Cornelius Low.

 The time of Gertrude, less than 2 years old, seemed brief, but her existence offered a blessing of lullabies and longing. She was the cherished daughter of Johanna and Cornelius Low.

 William, 8 years old, carried the promise of his father's name; life contained wonder and warmth. He was the beloved son of Johanna and Cornelius Low.

 Loomis, 3 years old, name resounding both legacy and love. He was the beloved son of Rhobie and John James Peck.

 James, 4 months old, though his period of existence was short, he remains a hallowed quiet in the family's story. He was the beloved son of Rhobie and John James Peck.

 Charlie, only lived less than a year, came and went like a breath, a lullaby never finished. He was the beloved son of Sarepta Ann and Frederick Peet.

 Bennie, 7 years old, and a youth of light, then flickered like a candle in the wind. He was the beloved son of Sarepta Ann and Frederick Peet.

 Dighton, under 1-year-old, his cradle closed before the world could call his name. He was the cherished infant son of Sarepta Ann and Frederick Peet.

 Margaret's presence briefly existed, but her name endures, a subtle mention within the family's narrative, a radiance that waned and extinguished quickly. She was the cherished daughter of Mary and Samuel Jr.

 G. Montrose, 3 months old, was an infant boy whose cradle swayed softly, keeping his memory in each still lullaby. He was the cherished infant son of Mary and Samuel Jr.

 Mary, only 2 years old, a daughter named for her mother, with her joy barely started. She was the cherished daughter of Mary and Samuel Jr.

 Robert, only 8 years old, was a son of bright spirit and gentle heart. He was the beloved son of Mary and Samuel Jr.

 Marguerite, only 5 years old, was the image of comfort and wonder as a child. She was the cherished daughter of Mary and Samuel Jr.

 Percy, only a month old, a newborn, was held for a fleeting time. He was the treasured infant son of Mary and Samuel Jr.

 Sally's cradle remained empty, though her presence was felt in every prayer. She was the precious infant daughter of Peninah and Richard Taylor.

 Obadiah, only 9 years old, once leaped through the fields, footsteps now remembered in the hush of twilight. He was the beloved son of Peninah and Richard Taylor.

 Sarah, 4 months old, lullaby lingers in the folds of visions. She was the precious infant daughter of Peninah and Richard Taylor.

 David, 12 years old, his name still reflects in the stories passed down, his absence a quiet ache. He was the treasured son of Peninah and Richard Taylor.

 Mary Malvina, almost 1-year-old, a baby girl whose name resembled her mother's. Her time was brief, remembered in every soft lullaby and quiet tear. She was the precious infant daughter of Peninah and Richard Taylor.

 Polly, five years old, was a precious child of joy and gentle spirit. She was the cherished daughter of Mercy and Captain Titus Watson.

 William arrived in silence, held in dreams. He was the treasured infant son of Mercy and Captain Titus Watson.

 Charles lived for 9 months. His cradle stood still too soon, but his presence lingers in every soft breeze. He was the cherished infant son of Louisa and George West.

 Infant Son [1] He was a son kept in faith, recalled in silence. He was the cherished infant son of Louisa and George West.

Infant Son [2] Another quiet goodbye. His name, though never stated, occupied a permanent position within the feelings of his parents, Louisa and George West.

 Howard, 5 years old, glee a thread woven through the quiet rhythms of home. Though his journey ended too soon, his memory remains, a tender light held close in the hearts that loved him. He was the beloved son of Harriet and John Westcot.

 Stephen's quiet flicker held close in the arms of love. Though he never saw the turning of seasons, his name remains, a tender reflection in the family's earliest prayers. He was the cherished infant son of Harriet and John Westcot.

 Seton, 5 years old, footsteps small but sure across the wooden floors of home. He was the beloved son of Emeline and David White.

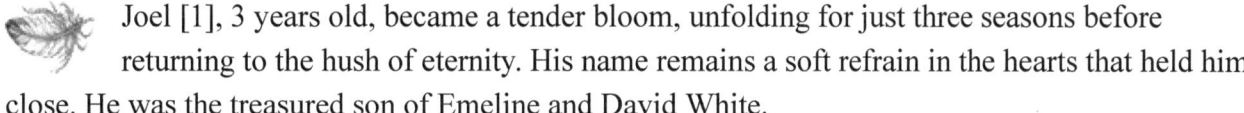 Joel [1], 3 years old, became a tender bloom, unfolding for just three seasons before returning to the hush of eternity. His name remains a soft refrain in the hearts that held him close. He was the treasured son of Emeline and David White.

 Joel [2], 9 years old, carried the name of his brother and the quiet strength of a second chance. Throughout his nine years, there was gentle resilience, a soul remembered for the light he brought and the quiet he left. He was the beloved son of Emeline and David White.

 The laughter of George "Georgie," only 2 years old, was a fleeting joy, a melody that danced through the halls before fading too soon. He was the revered son of Emeline and David White.

 Willie, one-year-old, a life presented a gentle breath, a single year of warmth held close in the arms of love. Though brief, his presence stitched a quiet sweetness into the family's unfolding story. He was the treasured infant son of Emeline and David White.

 Frederick "Fred," 11 years old, carried the spark of curiosity and kindness, a boy whose years glowed with promise. He was the beloved son of Emeline and David White.

 Infant Son, only lived less than a year, came like a whisper; a quiet blessing held for only a moment in time. Though unnamed in the records, his presence is etched in love, a cradle memory that never fades. He was the cherished infant son of Ada and Lanson Wiswall.

Infant Son was born into silence, carried in love. His name remained unsaid, yet his presence dwells peacefully in the hearts of those who waited. He was the cherished infant son of Eunice and Henry Wiswall.

# American Patriots

*In honor of all men and women who gave their lives for freedom, those loyal to country, liberty, and life.*

| Name | War |
|------|-----|
| Andrew Curtiss | Revolutionary War (1775 – 1783) |
| Brevet Brigadier General Ulysses Doubleday | Civil War (1861–1865) |
| Captain Edward Davis Thompson | Civil War (1861–1865) |
| Captain John Thompson | Revolutionary War (1775–1783) |
| Captain Reuben Westcot | War of 1812 (1812-1815) |
| Captain Stephen Ball | Revolutionary War (1775–1783) |
| Captain Stephen Horton | Civil War (1861–1865) |
| Captain Titus Watson | Revolutionary War (1775–1783) |
| Captain William McKittrick | Revolutionary War (1775–1783) |
| Colonel Elmer Ephraim Ellsworth | Civil War (1861–1865) |
| Colonel Ephraim Daniel Ellsworth | Civil War (1861–1865) |
| Colonel John Ball | Revolutionary War (1775–1783) |
| Colonel Thomas Donnelly Doubleday | Civil War (1861–1865) |
| David Walton Mabee | World War I (1914-1918) |
| Elisha Taylor | War of 1812 (1812-1815) |
| Ezekiel Horton | War of 1812 (1812-1815) |
| Frederick West | The Spanish-American War (April 21–August 13, 1898) |
| General James Gordon | Revolutionary War (1775–1783) |
| George Ellsworth | Civil War (1861–1865) |
| James Clark Horton | Civil War (1861–1865) |
| James Thompson | Civil War (1861–1865) |
| James Edward Holmes | Civil War (1861–1865) |

| Name | War |
| --- | --- |
| James Hodge Taylor | Indian Wars with the 5th Regiment Infantry |
| James Pitts | Civil War (1861–1865) |
| John Benjamin Ford | Civil War (1861–1865) |
| Major General Abner Doubleday | Civil War (1861–1865) War with Mexico (1846-1848) |
| Private William Horton | Civil War (1861–1865) |
| Roscoe Irving Wiswall | World War I (1914-1918) |
| Stephen S Horton | Revolutionary War (1775–1783) |
| Stephen Ward Doubleday | Civil War (1861–1865) |
| William Horton | Revolutionary War (1775–1783) |

# Ripples and Roots: An Evolution

*Here begins the quiet unfolding of a village, its waters stirred by labor, its soil deep with names. These timelines trace the pulse of Ballston Spa: the settlers who carved paths, the merchants who stitched commerce into daily life, the mills that hummed with purpose. Each ripple a moment, each root a memory.*

# The Molding of Towns

The Reverend Eliphalet Ball bought land from the MacDonald Brothers in 1785. Early settlers, the MacDonalds, resided near the area that's now called Ballston Lake. For ten shillings, the brothers sold the land, a humble amount that is worth less than a dollar now. Balls-Town, one of Saratoga County's "mother towns," was formed. Saratoga County was once part of Albany County for over 100 years. The city of Albany is much older than that, one of the oldest cities from the "New World."

The region developed outwards from this settlement's base. Balls-Town slowly became divided into smaller municipalities, towns, villages, and hamlets, which now make up a large part of present-day Saratoga County, New York.

The year 1791 saw the official formation of Saratoga County, carved from Albany County. Balls-Town, Halfmoon, Saratoga, and Stillwater were the first four settlements. To better manage its growth, Balls-Town was divided in a year. Milton and Galway appeared from their north and west sides. Charlton was carved out of the area's southwest corner.

Galway's town later gave rise to Providence and Edinburgh. Mechanicville became a city in 1915. In 1819 Saratoga Springs became a town, and later a city in 1915. Halfmoon established Clifton Park in 1828, and the name was changed from Clifton in 1829. In 1818, Corinth was founded in Hadley. Edinburg and Hadley were the basis for Day, formerly known as Concord, in 1819. The town was first called Northfield in 1801, but then it was renamed Edinburg in 1808. Greenfield's establishment in Milton and Saratoga occurred in 1793. In 1801, Hadley was erected in Greenfield and Northumberland. Northumberland brought forth Moreau in 1805.    Saratoga saw the founding of Northumberland in 1798. Waterford was constructed in Halfmoon and later became a village in 1816. Wilton was made in Northumberland in 1818.

In 1807, the village of Ballston Spa was founded in Ballston. Ballston Spa became the county seat permanently, even as Saratoga Springs grew. Kayaderosseras Creek's waterpower and mineral springs boosted tourism and industry, particularly in Ballston and Milton.

In 1802, Malta was formed, becoming independent of Stillwater. The shores of Saratoga and Round Lake were visited by the Mohawk and Mohegan peoples, the first inhabitants. The first Europeans built a settlement around a brewery, which became Maltaville, and then Malta.

The "daughter" towns:

- **Ballston** → Charlton, Galway, Milton (originally called Mill-Town, because of all the mills in the town)
- **Saratoga** → Northumberland, Malta, Saratoga Springs
- **Stillwater** → Malta, Mechanicville
- **Halfmoon** → Clifton Park, Waterford

Many Saratoga County town names reflect early settlers' origins, natural features, or symbolic aspirations. Some honor places in Scotland, England, Ireland, Greece and others derive from Indigenous languages, and a few are named after prominent families or ideals.

- Saratoga: From the Iroquois word *sah-rah-ka* or *sarach-togue*, meaning "the hill beside the river", referring to the Hudson River.
- Ballston: Named after the Ball family, early settlers who owned large tracts of land in the area.
- Charlton: Named after Charlton in England or Scotland, reflecting the heritage of early settlers.
- Galway: Named after Galway, Ireland, by Irish settlers who wanted to honor their homeland.
- Corinth: Named after the ancient Greek city, reflecting a classical naming trend popular in the early 1800s.
- Day: Named after Eliphaz Day, an early settler and influential figure in the town's formation.
- Edinburg: A variant spelling of Edinburgh, Scotland, chosen by Scottish settlers.
- Greenfield: Descriptive of the area's lush, open fields and forests.
- Halfmoon: Named for the crescent-shaped bend in the nearby Mohawk River.
- Moreau: Named after General Jean Victor Moreau, a French officer who visited the area.
- Northumberland: Named after the English county, reflecting British heritage.
- Providence: Reflects religious or spiritual aspirations of early settlers,
- Stillwater: Named for the calm waters of the Hudson River in that area.

- Waterford: Named after Waterford, Ireland, by Irish immigrants.

Every county, every town, every road leads somewhere, but they started somewhere. From the beginning, many towns and roads reflect legacies so they will not be forgotten. I hope that this book doesn't just give you information, but allows you to get to know your community, what it was, who lived here, and what it is now. Legacies can be light like feathers, blowing in the wind, or quiet and silent, with no one left who remembers.

Remember these people, I will, and I feel like I know them. And someday, I will be with them.

*Every life leaves a quantum footprint. May we never overlook its echo.*

# Appendix: Footnotes from the Field

*QR Codes to Echoes Beyond the Page*

*Here lie the scattered breadcrumbs of memory, links to timelines, cemetery tours, research notes, and shared kindness. Each code opens a door to the world beyond print, where Ballston breathes in quiet corners and history hums beneath the soil.*

*Research*

*Cemetery Research*

*Historical Articles*

*History of Balls-Town*

# Balls-Town: A Step Back in Time

***Balls-Town: A Community of History, Friends, Neighbors, and Lingering Spirits.***

Buy on Amazon:

https://essenceenterpriseus.com/

# References and Resources

Bradley, Leonard, Abram (1855) History of the Ball Family: Genealogy of the New Haven Branch. Privately Printed in NY (1916).

Gordon, J., & Mayer, J. (1936). Documents: The Reminiscences of James Gordon. New York History, 173, 316-333. http://www.jstor.org/stable/23135054 Grose, Edward F., Booth, John (1907) - Centennial History of the Village of Ballston Spa, including the town of Ballston and Milton-A souvenir of the Centennial Celebration, held June 22-25, (1907).

Mann, Enos (1876) The Bench and Bar of Saratoga County, https://play.google.com/books/reader?id=CK0sAAAAIAAJ&pg=GBS.PP10&hl=en

The Saratogian (1899) Our County and its People. A descriptive and biographical record of Saratoga County NY. Printed by The Boston History Company.

Sylvester, Nathaniel Bartlet (1876) Saratoga and Kayadrossera: An historical address.

Sylvester, Nathaniel Bartlett (1893) History of Saratoga County, New York; with historical notes of its various towns. Together with Biographical sketches of its prominent men and leading citizens.

Sylvester, Nathaniel Bartlett (1878) 1609-1878 History of Saratoga County New York with Illustrations and Biographical sketches. Some of its prominent men and pioneers.

**Family Genealogy Documents:**
Dunning Family Genealogy
Judge Taylor Descendants
Reminiscence of James Gordon
Thompson Family Genealogy

**Social Media:**
Amy Shannon YouTube Playlist for "History Comes Alive"

https://www.youtube.com/playlist?list=PLmJXg_2Jf1tji8kxaQK2nahoEaABHz6d5
Facebook Groups regarding Ballston Spa and outlining towns

**Local Resources:**

The Saratoga County Historical Society and Brookside Museum
21 Fairground Avenue Ballston Spa, NY 12020

Ballston Spa Village Cemetery Association
Archives of the Albany Academy for Girls (Portraits of Lucretia Booth, Betsey Colt Foot, and Ebenezer Foot).

**Other Online Resources:**

Ancestry website https://www.ancestry.com/
Ballston Spa Village Cemetery https://ballstonspacemetery.org/about/history/
Ballston Spa Village website https://www.villageofballstonspa.org/historical-sketch/pages/brief-history-ballston-spa
Find A Grave website https://www.findagrave.com/
Internet Archive website https://archive.org/
National Register of Historic Places https://nationalregisterofhistoricplaces.com/ny/saratoga/state.html
Saratoga County Historical Center https://brooksidemuseum.org/
Saratoga County Historical Roundtable website https://saratogacountyhistoryroundtable.com/books/
Genealogy Bank (Newspaper Archives) https://www.genealogybank.com/

# Titles Written by Amy Shannon

Amy's Short Story Collection
1) The Forsaken
2) Plan B
3) The Bridge of Shadows
4) The Backyard
5) Worth
6) G.O.D's Hands
7) My Final Chapter: A Legacy of Words
8) The Ultimate Short story Collection
9) My Final Chapter: A Legacy of Words
10 Red Ruby
11) Killer Lake
12) A Ghost's Writer
13) Mirror Realm
14) The Leather Legacy
15) Marcus and Lois

1980's
Algernon: Thief of the Poor
Who killed Mrs. Crane?
Flashback
The Midnight Ride

Flash Fiction
She
Emma

Interrogation
Retribution
Shadow
Light

Short Story Nonfiction
Mom
Gramma
Kerri
PTSD
Inward/Outward

Private Investigators Books
1) Passionate Retribution
2) Passionate Retribution 2
3) Passionate Retribution 3
4) Passionate Retribution 4
5) Passionate Retribution (Collection 1-4)
6) Fettering Shadows
7) Smashed
8) The Relic

Crime and Punishment Books
1) Fettering Shadows
8) Prowl
9) Preyfiler

Don't forget to pick up the Companion Cookbook Balls-Town: A Pioneer's Cookbook.

Please do the author a favor, and write a review where you purchased this book. Thank you.

Printed by Libri Plureos GmbH in Hamburg, Germany